MISSION-BASED MANAGEMENT

SECOND EDITION

AN ORGANIZATIONAL DEVELOPMENT WORKBOOK

PETER C. BRINCKERHOFF

A companion to the award-winning book
Mission-Based Management

JOHN WILEY & SONS, INC

New York • Chichester • Weinheim • Brisbane • Singapore • Toronto

WILEY NONPROFIT LAW, FINANCE, AND MANAGEMENT SERIES

NOTE TO THE READER:

All forms and material that were previously on a CD that accompanied this book have been moved to the following web site:

www.wiley.com/go/brinkerhoff

ISBN 0-471-39014-3

10 9 8 7 6 5 4 3 2 1

Contents

About the Author

Peter Brinckerhoff is an internationally acclaimed consultant, lecturer, and award-winning author. He is President of Corporate Alternatives, inc., the consulting firm that he founded in 1982. He is a former staff member, executive director, board member, and volunteer for local, state, and national not-for-profit organizations.

Peter is the author of five books on not-for-profit management issues, including the award-winning *Mission-Based Management*. His most recent book is *Social Entrepreneurship: The Art of Mission-Based Venture Development*.

Peter lives in Springfield, Illinois, with his wife and three children.

Preface

After the first edition of *Mission-Based Management* was published in 1994, I had many comments from readers about how they liked the practical nature of the book, and particularly the hands-on nature of the suggestions. As my other books were published, particularly the three that expanded on topics first raised in *Mission-Based Management*, I had the space to include more forms, formats, and checklists that helped readers implement my suggestions sooner. Through my training sessions I also have had the time to develop more hands-on self-assessments, more how-to forms, and more applications for participants who always come from widely varied backgrounds and with widely diverse skill levels.

As the second edition of *Mission-Based Management* was being contemplated, it became obvious that a companion volume was needed to help mission-based managers like you fully implement the suggestions, ideas, and concepts in the book. Thus this *Mission-Based Management: An Organizational Development Workbook*, which I sincerely hope will help you in your efforts to get more mission out of your organizational resources, sooner, in a higher quality manner, and to a more focused set of target markets.

I wish you the best in your reading, and in your application of the ideas in *Mission-Based Management*. I know, from long experience, that the ideas work, and that they result in better organizations doing more mission. Of course, not every idea works for every organization in every circumstance. Nor will any of the ideas serve as a panacea for a dysfunctional organization. But for most organizations in most situations the vast majority of the concepts and ideas can help you tremendously.

1

Introduction: How to Get the Most out of this Workbook

Welcome. This workbook is intended for the staff and board members of not-for-profit organizations as a hands-on tool to get more mission out the door, to help hone your organization's core competencies, to focus your resources, and in general to improve your overall mission capability. This workbook is really a tool to help you implement the ideas in *Mission-Based Management* in the easiest, quickest, and most efficient manner.

In this first chapter, I want to make sure that you understand how to get the most out of your investment in this workbook. I begin by making the assumption that you have read *Mission-Based Management*, preferably its second edition. While first edition readers will find excellent value in this workbook, they might be a bit confused by the chapter sequencing of the workbook, which is designed to coordinate with the second edition's updated list of key criteria of success for a mission-based organization.

That having been said, I assume that you want to get more out of *Mission-Based Management*, and that you want the tools to implement ideas from the book quickly and efficiently. If so, you've come to the right place. This workbook is filled with hands-on tools, checklists, forms, and displays to bring the concepts home and help you implement them in your organization smoothly, and as soon as possible.

To that end, let's start by going through the organization of the workbook and its chapters. Then I'll give you a few suggestions for using the tools included to the best effect.

A. ORGANIZATION

The chapter immediately following, on leading group discussions, is included because the absolute best way to implement ideas like the ones in *Mission-Based Management* is in teams. Thus, you or one of your management team is going to be doing a lot of group facilitation. Chapter 2 will help you get started if you have never done this, and hone your skills if you have.

Chapter 3 takes you through the next step: benchmarking. I've included a self-assessment form that will allow you to review your organization against my criteria for success, and even give yourself a preliminary grade in each area. Before you spend a lot of time and money implementing my ideas, make sure to take the time to benchmark. It will focus you on where your needs are the greatest, and motivate any members of your organization who do not think that there are ways to improve the organization.

Starting with Chapter 4 each chapter covers one main topic, and they coordinate with the corresponding numbered chapter in *Mission-Based Management*. The major components of each chapter are titled as follows:

Straight from *Mission-Based Management*

First we briefly review the key concepts included in *Mission-Based Management*. This will not only refresh your memory, but underscore the most important things to consider in the topic under discussion.

Baseline Self-Assessment

Even though you should have already completed a full organizational self-assessment, I include an expanded topic-specific assessment tool here for two reasons. First, the self-assessments in the chapters are more detailed, and offer you more potential avenues for improvement. Second, some readers will eschew the organization-wide self-assessment included in Chapter 3, and will only read the chapters that cover the topics of their most intense interest. The self-assessment tools in the chapters will also allow you to grade your organization on a scale to give you an overall sense of where your organization stands.

☞ **HANDS-ON:** In all of my books I include numerous practical suggestions highlighted by the ☞ **HANDS-ON:** icon so familiar to my readers. I have reiterated all the hands-on suggestions from each chapter in *Mission-Based Management* to give you some additional food for thought as you consider the best actions to take for your organization.

Worksheets and Checklists

The meat of the chapters will always be here. A series of worksheets and checklists will walk you through the steps of organizational improvement for each topic. Many of the worksheets will be self-explanatory. Where they are not, instructions will be included. Some of the worksheets stand alone, but many are provided in an intentional sequence, and build on one another, particularly in the areas of board development, social entrepreneurship, and strategic planning.

At the end of each chapter's group of forms and checklists is a blank implementation checklist to help you set deadlines for getting things done, and assigning people the responsibility for implementation.

Forms on the Companion CD-ROM

Most of the forms are also provided to you on the companion CD-ROM. This chart will list the form by form number, name, page, and file name on the CD-ROM. I urge you to print out copies of the forms in the book, or make duplicates from the book itself. Hopefully you will be working with a team, and you will want to have multiple copies. Also included on the CD-ROM are financial spreadsheets that you can use with Excel or

Lotus 1-2-3 for cash flow and income and expense projections. You will find these explained in the chapters on creating the social entrepreneur (Chapter 8) and financial empowerment (Chapter 10).

Resources for Further Study

In my books, I put the resources in the back, after the text. Here, I include them at the end of each chapter, to make it easier for you to focus on the topic at hand, and find more help if you need it.

B. HOW TO USE THE WORKBOOK

I have four suggestions on how to work your way through the workbook to the best effect. If efficient, effective outcomes are what you are looking for, consider these four as rules, not just suggestions.

1. Read *Mission-Based Management* First.

I know, I know, you want to get started. You don't have the time to read. But you need to understand that this workbook is designed as an implementation tool, not a complete reiteration of all of the background, examples, ideas, rationalizations, and encouragement in *Mission-Based Management*. If you want to "get it," read the book first.

2. Work as a Team.

As John Chambers, the CEO of Cisco Systems says, "No one of us is as smart as all of us." You are going to be suggesting change, sometimes very dramatic change, in your organization as a result of the ideas in this workbook. You need a team to realize that change. Using such a team to decide which ideas are for your organization, and enlisting the team's help in getting over the many barriers to implementation is the best way to proceed. The team should include your key management staff, but also representatives of your board of directors, and your mid-management and line staff. Nine to twelve people are about right for this group, with others being brought in for ad hoc input on areas of specific expertise.

3. Do the Self-Assessment as a Group.

For the workbook as a whole, and for each chapter in specific, start with the self-assessment. Make multiple copies and have the group fill them in independently. This assures more objectivity and reduces the likelihood of one strong member of the group skewing the assessments. Then, get back together and compile the assessments noting the range (the high and low) for each item, and the average.

Doing the self-assessment as a group will also give you a great opportunity for initial (and sometimes extended) discussion about the topic at hand. You will find out quickly about the perspectives of the group, and where more education or information dissemination on the topic is needed.

4. Set a Measurable Outcome, a Deadline for Implementation, and Assign Responsibility.

The last form in each chapter's section on forms and checklists is designed to help you here. As with any activity, if you don't set a measurable outcome, how can you tell if you succeeded? If you don't set a deadline, since work expands to fill the time allotted, you will never get done. And unless you tell an individual or group that an activity is their job, it will always be someone else's. Fill in the implementation form and enforce your expectations of outcome.

Here's another hint. If you move through the entire workbook, filling out all the implementation forms in each chapter, you will have a mission-based management action plan ready just by collating the forms and passing them out to your key staff and board! Then you can see how the organization can move ahead to be the mission-based business you need it to be.

As you move toward that goal, I wish you nothing but happy outcomes, and on sunny, low humidity days. But I know that that is not reality. Most readers are faced with many, many demands on their time, and many more mission-demands on their resources. You may well be highly stressed, distracted, and under a lot of pressure to make significant improvements in a short time. The workbook is designed to help just that kind of manager in just that kind of situation. By starting with the self-assessments, you can get a good idea of where you are. By using the forms and worksheets, you can detail specific outcomes and show progress in improving your organization. On crazy days, when it is hard to merely remember your name, much less have a creative idea, the checklists can focus your thoughts, and get you back on track.

And, you need to be on the track toward becoming that mission-based organization that you, your staff and board, and, most importantly, the people you serve need you to be. As always, mission is the bottom line. I hope that you find more mission outcomes result from your using this workbook. If so, we will both have done our jobs well. Good luck.

2

Leading Group Discussions:
A Primer

The core concept of this workbook is that you should use its forms, checklists, and decision trees to make progress in implementing ideas and suggestions from *Mission-Based Management* as a group. While managers need to have the capacity to make decisions on their own, most of the concepts in *Mission-Based Management* often require organizational changes of such large proportion that the best way to implement them is with a group.

In their good form, groups usually come up with consensus ideas. Groups can ameliorate ideas that are so radical that they are unworkable for an organization given its culture or its financial condition. Groups can share the workload and solve problems well. Remember John Chambers's quote from the first chapter, "No one of us is as smart as all of us." So very true.

Groups in their bad form can delay action, tear down new ideas, and force continuation of the same old, same old. They can protect turf, and turn really good, but a bit radical, ideas that will enhance mission into boring vanilla initiatives that will never motivate anyone.

Thus, as a leader of a mission-based organization, you need to be able to work with groups and get the good things out of them quickly, efficiently, and with at least a bit of consensus. This chapter will help you on that path.

A. STRAIGHT FROM *MISSION-BASED MANAGEMENT*

Three important ideas from *Mission-Based Management* pertain to this chapter:

1. The More Information People Have About the Organization the Better.

More than any other idea in the book, this pertains to the concept of including people in the decision-making process, and informing them of the outcomes of different committee deliberations. Don't try to do all the heavy lifting yourself. Include people from all levels of the organization on your mission-based management team, and inform everyone of the group's progress and deliberations. A number of my clients put the minutes of all their various staff and board committees on part of their website that can only be accessed by board and staff members. This lets staff keep up to speed on what is going on throughout the organization.

2. The Line Staff Are the Most Important Employees. Management Is a Support Function.

You need to use an inverted pyramid management style, where the most important people are the line staff. As part of that philosophy, as you implement my ideas, put people from your line staff, and representatives of your mid-management levels on your mission-based management team and do the same for your other committees. If line staff are important, get their input. And, if you want to grow your own stars internally, start now. Let them get a bigger picture of the organization by participating in bigger issues, learning how to be part of organizational leadership.

3. Mission-Based Managers Lead from the Front.

Yes, you need input. Yes, you need a group to give you a variety of perspectives. But, on some issues, after getting the input, you just have to make the decision and move ahead. In other words, lead. Examples of decisions you may have to make are: We *are* going to have a strategic plan. We *are* going to share our financial information widely. We *are* going to have two-way evaluations. We *are* going to think of all of our expenditures as investments. Once such decisions have been made, you can move the organization ahead. Max De Pree in his excellent book *Leading Without Power* notes that most not-for-profits "spend far too much time going for consensus rather than going for agreement." I concur completely. After you have your ideas, input, suggestions, and discussion, make the decision, and then ask: "We're going in such and such a direction. Are you coming with us?"

B. ASSEMBLING AND USING YOUR MISSION-BASED MANAGEMENT TEAM

1. A Mission-Based Management Implementation Process

In using this workbook, I would suggest that you use the following sequence of activity.

a. Assemble your mission-based management team.

I strongly recommend that you do two things with potential team members before you recruit them. First, talk to them privately to see if they are interested and enthusiastic about helping. Then, find out if they have major work conflicts that will keep them from attending meetings or getting their reading done on time. Make sure that they will be good team members. Second, don't select people just by title. Get the best people in your organization to work through these issues.

b. Read the appropriate chapter in Mission-Based Management.

You may want to do this chapter by chapter, or go through the entire workbook in a marathon session, and coordinate the activities intended to implement priority ideas from each chapter. I suspect you will get more out of your group if you go through a chapter at a time.

c. Meet and discuss the discussion questions at the end of each chapter.

Weekly meetings help to keep up the momentum. Certainly, you will lose your "mo" if you meet less than twice a month. Try to set all the meeting dates at the first session, and try for a consistent time and place (e.g., 2nd and 4th Mondays at 10:00 a.m.). Then, the team can have all the meetings on their calendar far in advance, and there will be less conflict.

d. Go through the forms and checklists in the workbook.

(Note that you are specifically allowed to copy these forms, and you can make originals from the accompanying disk.)

Make sure you copy all the forms on the CD-ROM before the meeting so that you can hand them out. Think about customizing the forms at the meeting to make them fit your needs better.

e. Fill out your Implementation Checklist (the final form in each chapter's section).

Some chapters have forms that are pretty all-inclusive. Others call for work that should go on your implementation checklist. In many cases you will think of things to improve that will not be on any of my lists. Make sure to include these tasks on this overall Implementation Checklist.

f. Monitor your progress toward completion.

As I have always said, process is important, but product is what you are shooting for. Set outcomes, set deadlines, assign responsibilities, and then enforce your expectations!

2. Rules for Facilitators

Most meetings need a leader or a facilitator. The facilitator of your meetings may or may not be the person that convenes the team and the meetings. A good facilitator is essential to getting the most out of the time that the team will spend together. Let's first review some key rules for facilitators, and them look at how they can be used in your meetings. (These come from Ron Myers, a strategic planning consultant based in New York.)

Ron's Rules:

1. Agree on the objectives of the meeting.
2. Establish a timeframe for the meeting.
3. Stick to the subject. Don't let people wander off the subject at hand, or the objectives and timeframe are both lost.

4. New input only. No repetition of old ideas, or ones that have already been discussed in the meeting.
5. Bottom line first. Focus on important matters. Fill in details later.
6. One conversation at a time. Squelch side conversations. Keep people focused on the speaker who has the floor.
7. No snide remarks.
8. Silence is consent. A person who does not speak up is assumed to consent to the group decision.

Ron also uses a great way to keep the group on track. Put a bowl in the middle of the table. Anyone who wanders off the subject, repeats something clearly said before, engages in a side conversation, or makes a snide remark puts money into the bowl. (The amount can vary: a quarter or a dollar.) The group as a whole is quick to call out when someone transgresses the rules. It serves to keep the group focused. The money is used to buy refreshments for the next meeting.

Now let's look at how these suggestions apply to your team.

1. Consider the choice of facilitator carefully. It may not be best to have the executive director or CEO be in charge of the meeting. You need someone who can move the discussion along, but not dominate the group. If the executive director is not the facilitator, the person who does the facilitating must be strong enough to cut the exec off if he or she starts to control the agenda.
2. Prior to the meeting, the facilitator must have thoroughly read the assignment, and should have reviewed the discussion questions suggested in *Mission-Based Management,* and the worksheets and checklists included in this workbook, and decided which to use. Any additional questions that may be important for the organization should also be written down. Copies of the questions to be asked should be distributed to members of the team. Also, any materials to be reviewed at the meetings (policies, mission statement, etc.) should be gathered prior to the meeting. Finally, the facilitator should assure that there is some means for writing down the work of the team. This may mean a chalk or white board, a flip chart, or someone taking notes.
3. At the beginning of each meeting, the facilitator should review the time allotted for the meeting, and what issues will be covered. The questions to be discussed can be distributed at this point, or the facilitator may want to simply ask the questions as the meeting progresses. This decision will depend on the facilitator's style. In any case, everyone should agree on the objectives of the meeting and the subjects to be discussed. A timeframe (deadline for adjournment) should also be reiterated. This should have been discussed in advance, but it never hurts to remind people.
4. The facilitator should start with the Key Philosophy and end with the Implementation Checklist for each chapter. This will focus and then wrap up the discussion well.
5. The facilitator should work to encourage discussion on all sides of an issue, and to assure that everyone present has a chance to voice their views. While the rules of facilitation above note that "silence is consent," I have found that there is always someone who wants to bring up the opposite view, but often they are

afraid. What I say is, "It seems we all agree that this is the way to go, but I am concerned that we haven't looked at the downside. What are the possible negative results of this action?" By doing this, I empower the person who would have been seen as a "nay-sayer." They have just been transformed from whiner to good manager. They get the chance to contribute and thus have ownership in the final decision. They also often bring up important ideas that the group would not have heard. Ultimately, however, if people are unwilling to contribute, they have consented to the will of the group.

Work to keep only new ideas on the table, and don't let people repeat the same ideas over and over, or make snide remarks about "wild ideas" that "won't work here." Use the bowl!

6. The facilitator should write down decisions and ideas developed by the group. I like using an easel and newsprint pad so that everyone can see what is being written down. This documents ideas and lets people brainstorm farther. Some facilitators like to have someone else as their "scribe" so that they can concentrate on keeping the group moving. Either way is fine.

7. Try to get through as many questions on the list as possible in each meeting, but don't go over the time allotted without complete concurrence from everyone there. For each question, focus on what changes or actions need to be taken to improve the organization, who should make them, and what deadline is appropriate. Again, remember that there is an implementation checklist provided in each chapter.

8. Remember, your meeting should probably not go more than 90 minutes. At the end of each session, reserve 10 minutes to review the decisions made, their deadlines, and who is responsible to make them happen. Have this written up and distributed in writing, by e-mail, or on your website to the participants within 24 hours. Remind everyone of the next meeting date and assignment before adjourning.

C. RESOURCES FOR FURTHER STUDY

Topic: Meeting Facilitation and Leadership

Books

Working Together: 55 Team Games, by Lorraine L. Ukens, Jossey-Bass, ISBN 0-7879-0354-X, 1996

The Skilled Facilitator: Practical Wisdom for Developing Effective Groups, by Roger M. Schwarz, Jossey-Bass, ISBN 1-55542-638-7, 1994

A Practical Guide to Needs Assessment, by Kavita Gupta, Jossey-Bass, ISBN 0-7879-3988-9, 1998

Software

Haven't seen any of this kind of software yet, but it won't be long, and perhaps even by the time you read this. Check on a site such as *www.downloads.com.*

Websites

The Chronicle of Philanthropy. Good management articles, and an annual resource directory: *www.philanthropy.com.*

PULSE! A bimonthly e-mail newsletter that features short articles on management, fund-raising, boards of directors, etc. To subscribe, send an e-mail message to: alliance@allianceonline.org that states in the body of the message "subscribe pulse!" Leave the subject blank, and do not leave an e-mail address in the body of the message.

On-Line Courses

Learning Institute for Nonprofit Organizations: *www.uwex.edu/li.* The Learning Institute provides live satellite training in a variety of subjects, including boards of directors, strategic planning, fund-raising, marketing, outcome measurement, social entrepreneurship, managing volunteers, etc. These courses are being put on the web as well.

3

Benchmarking Your Organization: A Baseline Self-Assessment Tool

So, let's get started. And first things first. I've provided you with a hands-on baseline assessment tool that will help you and your mission-based management team take an initial look at the status of your organization in relation to my criteria for success and my suggestions in the book. Take the time to fill in this survey as a group, *now*. Then you can focus your efforts on the parts of your organization that can most benefit from your time and efforts.

A. STRAIGHT FROM *MISSION-BASED MANAGEMENT*

I just have to give you the three big philosophies again before we get started. You need to read these aloud as a group and talk them through. If your mission-based management team agrees on these, you are going to make excellent changes. If there is disagreement about the underlying concepts below, you need to know it *before* you start, not after. *Mission-Based Management* hinges on these three ideas:

1. Your Organization Is a Mission-Based Business.

Your organization is in the business of mission. Making money is important, but mission is always first. You, your staff, and your volunteers are all stewards of your mission, charged with getting the most mission you can from all your resources. Some of those resources are business techniques that can be applied to mission, such as marketing, cash management, and benchmarking, as we will do in this chapter. If it can result in more mission, use it!

2. No One Gives Your Organization a Dime.

You earn all your income, even charitable donations. Why? Because you give people something for your money. When someone donates to your organization, he or she is really purchasing services for someone they will never meet. Don't accept the idea that you get subsidies. You don't. Subsidies are things people get for doing nothing. You do something for your money. You earn it all.

3. It's Perfectly Legal (and a Really Good Thing) to Make Money.

Making money in a not-for-profit is a good thing, not a bad thing. Why? Because only by making money can you innovate, try new services, grow your organization, and take reasonable risks on behalf of the people you serve. You don't have to make money with every service you provide, but overall, in most years, the organization should have more money at the end of the year than it did at the beginning.

B. BASELINE SELF-ASSESSMENT

To make plans for the future, you must know where you are in the present. These self-assessment pages are designed to help you, your staff, and your board diagnose the current situation of your organization in relation to my suggestions and ideas in *Mission-Based Management*. The sections follow the chapters in the book.

This self-assessment tool can be used in many ways. One of the best ways is to conduct a retreat or workshop involving key organization leaders. Or use it at the first meeting of your mission-based management team. At the session, provide each participant with the self-assessment pages and a copy of *Mission-Based Management*. Then begin the session by going through the self-assessment (referring to the book as needed). Invite open discussion. Encourage an honest and fair assessment. Don't squelch the negative assessments. After all, no organization can be perfect. The self-assessment discussion will be helped by having a large pad of paper on an easel or a chalk board. The facilitator can write down comments that indicate areas needing attention. And, you can score your organization and see where you need the most improvement. If you score on the low side in a certain section, don't panic! Set some goals for short-term improvement.

Remember, each of the most critical items should be assigned to a person to follow through on. A timetable should be established for each item using Form 3-2. This list of top priority items, the person responsible for each, and the date or dates for taking the key steps to deal with the item should be recorded. This list will be a record of the outcomes of the session, outcomes that will lead to actions in areas where the organization's leaders have diagnosed a need for improvement through this self-assessment.

Instructions: Go through each area of the self-evaluations (Forms 3-1 to 3-9). For each question, circle the box with the score next to the question. Then total your scores in each column, add the Yes and No columns together, and put the resulting TOTAL SCORE in the appropriate box for each subject. A score can be positive, negative, or 0. For example, if you have a yes answer for the first question under mission statement, you get a 2. A no answer gets a −2. A "perfect" mission would generate a score of 13. A −5 would be generated if all the answers were No.

Form 3-1 Self-Assessment—Mission Statement (Chapter 4)		
	Yes	**No**
Has your mission statement been reviewed by your board and staff within the past two years?	2	–2
Does staff use the mission statement as an aid to decision-making and management? Are copies on the table at every meeting?	3	–1
Does the board refer to the mission statement when considering adding or dropping services? Are copies on the table at every meeting?	3	–1
Is your mission statement posted in the organization? Included in marketing materials? Stated in personnel policies?	2	–1
Is the mission statement used as a criteria in your personnel evaluations?	3	0
Total of column score Add each column up and put the answer here ➜		
TOTAL SCORE—MISSION Add total scores from Yes and No columns and put the answer here ➜		

● CH0301.DOC

Form 3-2 Self-Assessment—Board of Directors (Chapter 5)

	Yes	No
Does the board have a mandated policy of turnover? (Are there set terms for board members? A limit on the number of consecutive terms?)	3	–3
Is there an annual assessment of the skills of board members? Is that list compared to a list of skills needed on the board this year and within the next three years?	2	0
Does the board have a written list of its responsibilities?	2	–2
Have more than 75% of board meetings had a quorum over the past 24 months?	3	–4
Is there a current, written board manual?	1	–1
Does the board annually evaluate the head staff person, in person and in writing?	3	–3
Is the board involved in strategic planning on a consistent and regular basis?	2	0
Is time set aside at each board meeting for ongoing orientation about the organization's work?	2	0
Does the board annually approve the budget and then monitor it on a regular basis?	3	–5
Total of column score Add each column up and put the answer here ➜		
TOTAL SCORE—BOARD OF DIRECTORS Add total scores from Yes and No columns and put the answer here ➜		

 CH0302.DOC

Form 3-3 Self-Assessment—Staff Management (Chapter 6)

	Yes	No
Does the organization chart and culture place the people that the organization serves in the primary (top) position?	3	–1
Are staff who directly provide service included in budget development and other decisions?	3	–1
Do staff from all levels of the organization serve on most staff committees?	2	0
Are staff evaluations done at least annually?	3	–2
Are all staff provided training and/or continuing education at least 10 hours per year per person above any training needed for licensure or accreditation?	3	0
Are staff encouraged to innovate and take risks?	2	0
Do the staff formally evaluate their supervisors?	2	–1
Does staff have both responsibility and authority to meet service needs?	3	–1
Is there a staff recognition program? Was it designed by staff (not management)?	1	–1
Total of column score Add each column up and put the answer here ➜		
TOTAL SCORE—MANAGEMENT Add total scores from Yes and No columns and put the answer here ➜		

CH0303.DOC

Form 3-4 Self-Assessment—The Wired Not-for-Profit (Chapter 7)

	Yes	No
Do we consider technology an important investment?	3	–1
Does the organization have a website? Has it been updated in the past 30 days?	4	–3
Does the organization have e-mail for board members?	2	–2
Are all the organization's computers Net compatible?	2	–1
Does the organization do a quarterly (four times a year) technology assessment?	3	0
Does the organization have a single staff (or volunteer) who is responsible for technological upkeep and updating?	2	–1
Do staff get access to classes in software and hardware use?	2	–2
Does the organization have e-mail for all staff?	3	0
Does the organization subscribe to one periodical that covers not-for-profit technological issues?	1	–1
Total of column score Add each column up and put the answer here ➔		
TOTAL SCORE—WIRED Add total scores from Yes and No columns and put the answer here ➔		

● CH0304.DOC

Form 3-5 Self-Assessment—Social Entrepreneurship (Chapter 8)

	Yes	No
Has the organization investigated (or is currently pursuing) non-traditional business activities to supplement income?	3	0
Does the organization weigh the mission return and the financial return of every investment (and view expenditures as investments)?	3	0
Are program options or change opportunities free of restriction from facilities or debt you already have?	2	–2
Are the concerns of staff and service recipients acknowledged and addressed when change is initiated?	2	0
Are core values and the mission statement discussed when changes are considered?	2	–3
Have you discussed with board and staff the organizational willingness to take risk?	2	0
Is change initiated as an improvement without criticizing what has been done before?	1	0
Total of column score Add each column up and put the answer here ➔		
TOTAL SCORE—SOCIAL ENTREPRENEURSHIP Add total scores from Yes and No columns and put the answer here ➔		

 CH0305.DOC

Form 3-6 Self-Assessment—Marketing (Chapter 9)

	Yes	No
Have you identified your organizational target markets for finders, people to serve, and referrers?	3	–3
Have all your staff had customer satisfaction training in the past year?	2	–1
Have you asked your target markets what they want, or how satisfied they are with your services in the past 24 months?	3	–1
Are your marketing materials targeted to individual markets?	2	–1
Have your marketing materials been updated in the past 18 months?	1	–1
Do you empower your staff members to fix customers' problems promptly?	2	–2
Are you constantly trying to improve your services from your customers' point of view?	2	0
Has your website been reviewed and updated within the past 60 days?	2	0
Do you have a current marketing plan?	1	0
Total of column score Add each column up and put the answer here ➜		
TOTAL SCORE—MARKETING Add total scores from Yes and No columns and put the answer here ➜		

● CH0306.DOC

Form 3-7 Self-Assessment—Financial Empowerment (Chapter 10)

	Yes	No
Do you have 30 days cash on hand?	2	0
Has your organization been profitable in the past three years?	3	0
Do you have financial policies that have been updated in the past 18 months?	2	−3
Do you know which of your programs make money and which lose money?	2	0
Do you have an endowment?	1	0
Do you and your board view your expenditures as investments?	2	0
Do you involve staff in budget development?	1	−1
Do you involve staff in budget implementation?	2	−1
Do you share your financial information widely inside the organization?	2	−1
Do you have a banker with whom you meet regularly?	1	0
Do you have a line of credit?	2	0
Total of column score Add each column up and put the answer here ➔		
TOTAL SCORE—FINANCIAL EMPOWERMENT Add total scores from Yes and No columns and put the answer here ➔		

CH0307.DOC

Form 3-8 Self-Assessment—Planning (Chapter 11)

	Yes	No
Do you have a current strategic plan (3 to 5 years)?	**4**	**–2**
Are both board and staff involved in the strategic planning process?	**3**	**–2**
Do you float drafts of your plan widely both inside and outside the organization?	**3**	**–1**
Does your planning process include the people you serve, the funding sources, and the community?	**3**	**–3**
Do you regularly review progress at implementing the strategic plan at staff and board meetings?	**2**	**0**
Total of column score Add each column up and put the answer here ➔		
TOTAL SCORE—PLANNING Add total scores from Yes and No columns and put the answer here ➔		

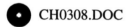 CH0308.DOC

Form 3-9 Self-Assessment—Controls (Chapter 12)

	Yes	No
Do you have the following policies, and have they been updated within the past 24 months?		
Bylaws	3	–3
Conflict of Interest	2	–2
Financial Policies	2	–3
Personnel Policies	2	–3
Media Policies	2	–1
Quality Assurance Policies	2	0
Do you train staff and board annually on key policies?	2	0
Do you enforce your policies consistently?	3	–2
Total of column score Add each column up and put the answer here ➜		
TOTAL SCORE—CONTROLS Add total scores from Yes and No columns and put the answer here ➜		

CH0309.DOC

Form 3-10 Self-Assessment—Score Compilation

Instructions: Review your earlier scoring. Transfer the score for each area, and then sum your total self-assessment score at the bottom of the form.

Area	Your Score	Possible Score
Mission		13
Boards		22
Staff Management		22
The Wired Not-for-Profit		22
Social Entrepreneurship		15
Marketing		18
Financial Empowerment		20
Planning		15
Controls		18
Total Self-Assessment Score:		165

● CH0310.DOC

Remember, this is just an initial assessment. You will use the remainder of the workbook to go into more detail in each area, and I have included suggestions and checklists for each topic to help you improve your score, and your overall mission-capability. Keep a copy of this score, and when you are done with the workbook, come back and do the self-assessment again. I'm sure you will see big improvements!

C. FORMS ON THE COMPANION CD-ROM

Form Name	Form #	Workbook Page	File Name	File Format
Self-Assessment—Mission Statement	3-1	13	CH0301.DOC	Word for Windows
Self-Assessment—Board of Directors	3-2	14	CH0302.DOC	Word for Windows
Self-Assessment—Staff Management	3-3	15	CH0303.DOC	Word for Windows
Self-Assessment—The Wired Not-for-Profit	3-4	16	CH0304.DOC	Word for Windows
Self-Assessment—Social Entrepreneurship	3-5	17	CH0305.DOC	Word for Windows
Self-Assessment—Marketing	3-6	18	CH0306.DOC	Word for Windows
Self-Assessment—Financial Empowerment	3-7	19	CH0307.DOC	Word for Windows
Self-Assessment—Planning	3-8	20	CH0308.DOC	Word for Windows
Self-Assessment—Controls	3-9	21	CH0309.DOC	Word for Windows
Self-Assessment—Score Compilation	3-10	22	CH0310.DOC	Word for Windows

D. RESOURCES FOR FURTHER STUDY

Topic: Self-Assessment—General Management

Books

The Drucker Foundation Self-Assessment Tool: Process Guide, by Peter Drucker, Gary Stern, and Francis Hesselbien, Jossey-Bass, ISBN 0-7879-4436-X, 1998

Evaluation with Power: Developing Organization Effectiveness, by Sandra Trice Gray, Jossey-Bass, ISBN 0-7879-0913-0, 1997

Reengineering Your Nonprofit Organization: A Guide to Strategic Transformation, by Alceste T. Pappas, John Wiley & Sons, ISBN 0-471-11807-9, 1995

Mission-Based Management Audio Tapes, by Peter Brinckerhoff. Available at *www.missionbased.com.* A six-tape, twelve-side set—excellent to orient busy board members to the key tenets of *Mission-Based Management.*

Software

I've not seen any of this other than that tied to continuous quality improvement. Again, check around. I wouldn't be a bit surprised if some existed by the time you read this.

Websites

Organizational Performance Management: *www.mapnp.org/library/org_perf/org_perf.htm.* Good self-assessment information from Carter McNamara and the Free Management Site.

I've also used this initial self-assessment chapter to provide you with general web resources for not-for-profits.

The Nonprofit FAQ: *www.nonprofit-info.org/npofaq/index.html*

Discussion Newsgroup: *soc.org.nonprofit*

The Nonprofit Risk Management Center: *www.nonprofitrisk.org*

Independent Sector: *www.indepsec.org*

Society for Nonprofit Organizations: *www.uwex.edu/li*

Nonprofit Gateway: *www.nonprofit.gov*

IRS Information on Tax-Exempt Organizations: *www.irs.ustreas.gov/prod/bus_info/eo*

Compasspoint: *www.compasspoint.org*

Innonet: *www.innonet.org*

On-Line Courses

Learning Institute for Nonprofit Organizations: *www.uwex.edu/li.* The Learning Institute provides live satellite training in a variety of subjects, including boards of directors, strategic planning, fund-raising, marketing, outcome measurement, social entrepreneurship, managing volunteers, etc. These courses are being put on the web as well.

4

The Mission Is the Reason

A. STRAIGHT FROM *MISSION-BASED MANAGEMENT*

Here's the key material from Chapter 4 in *Mission-Based Management*. My point in reminding you and your mission-based management team about this is to focus you before you start implementing your ideas on the point (the mission) and to help you focus your organization on better mission *now*, not later, after all the other changes have been made.

1. The Mission Is the Reason

The mission statement is your organization's reason for being. It is, of course, the foundation of your corporate status (you couldn't get a not-for-profit status from your state or your 501(c) designation from the Internal Revenue Service without it), but also it should be the final outcome of all your organizational actions. The first rule of not-for-profits is: *Mission, mission, and more mission!*

2. The Mission Is an Underutilized Resource

Most organizations don't get enough good out of their mission statement. It is not fully used as a resource for policy setting, management, recruitment, retention, or fundraising. Good stewards get the most they can out of their mission statement. Does your organization?

B. BASELINE SELF-ASSESSMENT

Note: This self-assessment includes the questions you answered in Chapter 3, plus a number of new ones. Go through and score your organization as best you can. Do this assessment as a group, if possible, or individually, and then collate your scores.

Form 4-1 Mission Statement Self-Assessment

	Yes	No
Has your mission statement been reviewed by your board and staff within the past two years?	2	–2
Ask five staff at random what the mission statement is. Do all five get reasonably close?	4	–1
Ask four board members what the mission statement is. Do all four get reasonably close?	4	–1
Does staff use the mission statement as an aid to decision-making and management? Are copies on the table at every meeting?	3	–1
Is there a vision statement associated with your mission statement?	2	0
Is the mission statement short—less than 50 words?	4	–2
Does the board refer to the mission statement when considering adding or dropping services? Are copies on the table at every meeting?	3	–1
Do you celebrate the success of your mission at every staff meeting?	3	–1
Do staff and board consider, and verbalize, that expenditures are really investments in mission?	2	–1
Is your mission statement posted in the organization? Included in marketing materials? Stated in personnel policies?	2	–1
Is the current mission statement on file with the IRS?	3	–3
Is the mission statement used as a criteria in some manner in your personnel evaluations?	3	0
Total of column score Add each column up and put the answer here ➔		
TOTAL SCORE—MISSION STATEMENT Add total scores from Yes and No columns and put the answer here ➔		

 CH0401.DOC

SCORING ANALYSIS:

34–27 Excellent
26–20 Very Good
19–10 Adequate
Less than 10—You are not getting the benefit you should out of this resource.

As you look at your mission, remember that you want it to be short, exciting, motivating, and descriptive of what you do and the world you want to live in.

C. WORKSHEETS AND CHECKLISTS

Here are some things you can do to improve your mission statement:

Form 4-2 Mission Statement Checklist	
____	Review your mission statement at the management level. Ask these questions:
	Does the mission use correct, current language?
	Does the mission describe adequately who we serve? (demographics)
	Does the mission describe adequately where we work? (geographics)
	Does the mission show focus?
	Does the mission excite us?
	Can we get our mission down to less than 50 words?
	Do we need a vision associated with our mission?
	Do we need to write down a statement of values along with our mission?
____	Ask the staff to discuss not just the mission statement wording, but what it means to them.
____	Meet with the board and staff, discuss your findings, and talk about necessary changes.
____	Any adopted changes should be sent to the IRS with details of the board meeting, and a listing of the board members who voted for and against the changes.
____	The mission statement should be evident everywhere: On the wall, on marketing materials, on the back of staff business cards, on screen savers, on the annual report, on the table at board and staff meetings.

● CH0402.DOC

Use this form to write down the things you need to do from the checklist on the previous page.

Form 4-3 Implementation Checklist Topic: Mission		
Measurable Outcome	**Deadline**	**Person or Group Responsible**

● CH0403.DOC

D. ☞ HANDS-ON

Here are the ☞ **HANDS-ON** ideas from Chapter 4 of *Mission-Based Management:*

☞ **HANDS-ON:** Once the mission is reviewed and rewritten, have it formally adopted by the board of directors or voted on by your membership (meeting whatever stipulations are in the bylaws) *and then send it, with the minutes of the board action to your state attorney general and to the Internal Revenue Service.* This is critical, as the IRS will judge you under the Unrelated Business Income Tax provisions of the Code based on the mission statement that they have *on file.* If you don't send the amended mission statement to the IRS, they will never know, and will judge you on your old, outdated mission statement.

☞ **HANDS-ON:** Try this: At your next board meeting, and next senior management meeting, ask everyone to get a piece of paper out and write down in one sentence *the single* *most important thing your organization does.* Now have everyone read their answers off and write them on the board, or on a flipchart. Compare the answers. How many duplications do you have? If you are like the overwhelming number of not-for-profits, you'll have few if any duplications. Why? Because *everyone* in the organization comes to it from a different background, perspective, or priority.

☞ **HANDS-ON:** Try this: When the going gets particularly tough, when morale is low, or it seems people have given up hope, ask your staff or your board to list the good things that have happened in the last three weeks or months as a result of your organization being in business. Get personal, talking about the impact of your organization's services on individuals. Then turn it around, and ask them what would have happened if you hadn't been around as an organization. Refocus on the mission statement as a higher calling, a cause worth working and sacrificing for. Note: You can't use this exercise every day, as it will lose its impact. Save it for when you *really* need it.

E. FORMS ON THE COMPANION CD-ROM

Form Name	Form #	Workbook Page	File Name	File Format
Mission Statement Self-Assessment	4-1	26	CH0401.DOC	Word for Windows
Mission Statement Checklist	4-2	27	CH0402.DOC	Word for Windows
Implementation Checklist	4-3	28	CH0403.DOC	Word for Windows

F. RESOURCES FOR FURTHER STUDY

Topic: Mission

Books

Surprisingly, when you do a book search, you come up dry in the not-for-profit world, where mission is so critical. Here are three books targeted at the for-profit world that might be worth a quick review.

The Path: Creating Your Mission Statement for Work and for Life, by Laurie Beth Jones, Hyperion, ISBN 0786882417, 1998

The Mission Statement Book: 301 Corporate Mission Statements for America's Top Companies, by Jeffrey Abrahams, Ten Speed Press, ISBN 180081320, 1999

Say It and Live It: 50 Corporate Mission Statements that Hit the Mark, by Patricia Jones and Larry Kahaner, Doubleday, ISBN 0385476302, 1995

Software

None that I am aware of here. But. . .

Websites

None that I am aware of at this time, except for the hilarious mission generator at *www.dilbert.com.* No, you can't use it for your own mission statement. But it will give you a chuckle.

On-Line Courses

Learning Institute for Nonprofit Organizations: *www.uwex.edu/li.* The Learning Institute provides live satellite training in a variety of subjects, including boards of directors, strategic planning, fund-raising, marketing, social entrepreneurship, managing volunteers, etc. These courses are being put on the web as well.

5

A Businesslike Board of Directors

A. STRAIGHT FROM *MISSION-BASED MANAGEMENT*

As you start working on your board issues, remember to include board members in your deliberations about this issue, particularly about recruitment and evaluation. Think of them as an essential market. Ask them what they *want* from their board service. Here are some key tenets from *Mission-Based Management* to try to operate by.

Your Board Is a Key and, Too Often, Underutilized Resource.

You have to have a board of directors that is in charge of a not-for-profit. As that is the case, get the most out of them. Find good board members, orient them constantly, give them the support they require, and try your best to retain them for their full board term of service. Don't look at the board as a burden, but as a current (or at least as a potential) resource.

You Need Lots of Skills on Your Board, but Two Main Kinds of People.

Boards need many skills, but two major backgrounds. The first group are what I call *advocates*, people who passionately believe in the mission of the organization. These people keep you focused on the first rule of not-for-profits which is: "Mission, mission, and more mission!" The second group of people are businesspeople, folks who understand the business cycle, marketing, cash flow, human resources, and the like. These vital individuals keep the organization focused on the second rule of not-for-profits which is: "No money, No mission!" Having both of these kinds of people on your board in a reasonable balance provides the group with a dynamic tension which is good for the board, the organization, and the people you serve.

A Board Is a Market Like any Other. You Need to Find Out What They Want Out of Their Service and Give It to Them.

Too often, we are happy if our board members just attend the board meeting. Thus we don't worry about making the meeting very interesting, or even particularly valuable. We fear that, if we give the board too much to do, they won't come. The problem with that is that you want the best board people possible, and won't get them if they are bored.

Board members want to feel needed, appreciated, and know that their work has meaning. At least most boards do. What about yours? Have you asked them recently?

Boards Should Deal with Policy, Not with Day-to-Day Management.

Boards (except during start-up, extreme financial crisis, and if there is a scandal in the executive director's position) need to stick to policy, and leave the management to the staff. Policy items include planning, budgeting, decisions on new services, new locations, debt, adoption of personnel, financial, and other policies.

The Executive Director (By any Name) Works for the Board. All of the Other Staff Work for the Executive Director.

The traditional term for this is chain of command. While staff should absolutely work *with* the board (staffing committees and the like), both board and staff need to respect the need to go through the head staff person, and not around him or her, unless there is something illegal or immoral occurring.

B. BASELINE SELF-ASSESSMENT

Form 5-1 Board of Directors Self-Assessment

	Yes	No
Does the board have a mandated policy of turnover? (Are there set terms for board members? A limit on the number of consecutive terms?)	3	–3
Is there an annual assessment of the skills of board members?	2	0 .
Is that list compared annually to a list of skills needed on the board this year and within the next three years?	2	0
Does the board have these skills represented?		
Legal	1	0
Business	1	0
Financial	1	0
Marketing	1	0
Fund-Raising	1	0
Human Resources	1	0
Does the organization carry director's and officer's insurance?	2	0
Does the board have a written list of its responsibilities?	2	–2
Have more than 75% of board meetings had a quorum over the past 24 months?	3	–4
Is there a current, written board manual?	1	–1
Does the board have standing committees that function regularly?	2	0
Do board members receive their meeting information at least three days before each meeting?	2	0
Does the board have and enforce a conflict of interest policy?	3	0
Are board members actively involved in fund-raising?	3	0
Do all board members contribute to the organization annually?	3	–2
Does the board annually evaluate the head staff person, in person and in writing?	3	–3
Is the board involved in strategic planning on a consistent and regular basis?	2	0
Is time set aside at each board meeting for ongoing orientation about the organization's work?	2	0
Does the board annually approve the budget and then monitor it on a regular basis?	3	–5
Total of column score Add each column up and put the answer here ➜		
TOTAL SCORE—BOARD OF DIRECTORS Add total scores from Yes and No columns and put the answer here ➜		

● CH0501.DOC

44–34 Excellent
33–22 Very Good
21–13 Adequate
Less than 13—You are not getting the benefit you should out of this resource.

Think through your board issues carefully, including both board and staff. Here you may well want to prioritize within the area, taking the issues that are most critical and/ or the ones that will cause the least political trouble first. Remember, your board is a market: What do they want?

C. WORKSHEETS AND CHECKLISTS

Form 5-2 Board of Directors Checklist	
_____	Review your readiness in these areas:
	Is our board manual up to date?
	Is our conflict of interest policy up to date?
	Do we know what percentage of our board members complete their full term? What is the trend in this area over time?
	Have we reviewed the conflict of interest policy with the board in the past 12 months?
	Do we have all the board members we need? (see Form 5-3)
	Do we have a regular board orientation program?
—	Ask the board to discuss not just the mission statement wording, but what it means to them.
—	Has the board evaluated the executive director in the past 12 months?
—	If you haven t had one in the past 24 months, consider a board planning retreat.
—	Consider getting your board trained through the National Center for Nonprofit Boards, through your trade association, or through a private consultant. This training can be on appropriate board roles, board fund-raising, use of committees, etc.

● CH0502.DOC

Fill in this sheet, looking at your current board, and forecasting when you will need new board members.

Form 5-3 Board Composition Assessment Sheet					
Characteristic/ Expertise	On Board	We Need this Skill			
		Now	1 Year	2 Years	3 Years
Gender					
Ethnicity (Various)					
Funder's Mandate (Required by a Funder)					
Age Group (Various)					
Location (County, City, Etc.)					
Advocate					
Legislative					
Clergy					
Current or Former Customer					
Fund-Raising					
Legal					
Accounting					
Finance/Banking					
Marketing					
Personnel					
Construction					
Building Management					
Small Business					

CH0503.DOC

Use this as a guide to develop a survey form to find out what your board members want from their service on your organization.

Form 5-4 Sample Board Survey

1. Why did you agree to serve on our board?
   Because I or a family member have used the organization s services.
   Because I want to contribute back to my community.
   Because I ve always wanted to serve on a board.
   Other _____

2. What is the best part about serving on our board?
   The meetings.
   My fellow board members.
   Feeling like I am contributing.
   The services our organization provides.
   The information from the staff.
   Other _____

3. What is the worst part about serving on our board?
   The meetings.
   My fellow board members.
   Feeling like I am contributing.
   The services our organization provides.
   The information from the staff.
   Other _____

4. What information would you like to see that you are now not getting regularly?

5. What information that you are now getting regularly would you suggest discontinuing?

6. On what aspect of the organization would you like more information/training?

7. If there could be one change that would improve your satisfaction as a board member, what would it be?

● CH0504.DOC

Use this form to write down the things you need to do from the checklist on the previous page, or to list other key issues to resolve.

Form 5-5 Implementation Checklist	Topic: Board of Directors	
Measurable Outcome	**Deadline**	**Person or Group Responsible**

● CH0505.DOC

D. ☞ HANDS-ON

☞ **HANDS-ON:** At *every* board meeting, reserve 15 minutes for ongoing board orientation. Cover a single program, a new state law affecting your organization, or new developments in your field. Orientation should be a continuous, never-ending process. Too often it is only done at one meeting at the beginning of the board member's term, provided in a language (your jargon) that the board member does not yet understand. Think back to your own orientation when you joined your employer's staff. How much do you remember? Not much, and you have worked there 40 hours a week ever since. Now add to that only "working" 3 to 4 hours a month as a board member does, and you may get the picture about why they don't keep 100% up to speed. Help them keep current by dedicating 15 minutes per meeting. (If you don't think you have 15 minutes, see the section of this chapter that deals with more effective committee meetings.)

☞ **HANDS-ON:** You also need a tool to help you entice by enforcement. All boards should have attendance requirements that are discussed during recruitment, and enforced rigorously. For example, if you have 12 meetings a year, each board member must come to a minimum of 9 per year, or not be renewed for membership. Missing three in a row is cause for probation with one more miss leading to termination. If this sounds tough, it is designed to be. You are a mission-oriented business and you can't get your business done without board attendance. Be up front with your board people and let them know you can no longer have them be casual about attendance. They need to be on or off the board, not both. Board members are liable for actions taken at meetings that they miss. That fact alone should entice them to come to meetings.

☞ **HANDS-ON:** You need a huge and varied skillset on a board, but at its core, a businesslike board should have two broad categories of members. First, you need advocates for your mission—people who passionately believe in what you do. These people keep you honest to the first rule of not-for-profits which is, "Mission, mission, and more mission!" The second kind of people you need are businesspeople, and these folks keep you honest to the second rule of not-for-profits: "No money, no mission! These two groups provide a dynamic and very healthy tension on the board, and help the organization balance the needs of the two primary rules.

☞ **HANDS-ON:** One technique that I have seen work is to assign a senior staff person, not the Executive Director, and one veteran board member to each new board member as their "buddies" for six months. These people sit with the new member at the meetings, take them to lunch once or twice to check on whether they are getting what they need, are available by phone to chat, etc. It's a method to increase the likelihood of meeting the new member's wants and assuring that problems or questions are resolved early. This buddy system does not need to last long (three to six months) but it really works.

☞ **HANDS-ON:** Some board members will not be happy with their committee assignments. One way to solve this is to ask board members which committee they would prefer to serve on before the decision is made. At the last board meeting of the year, provide each board member with a written checklist of available committee assignments that must be returned to the president by the deadline noted. (Make it clear that it is not always possible to place them on the committee of their choice, but every effort will be made to do so. If they do not submit the form by the deadline noted, their assignment will be made by the president.) Then based on this and the organization's needs, make assignments.

E. FORMS ON THE COMPANION CD-ROM

Form Name	Form #	Workbook Page	File Name	File Format
Board of Directors Self-Assessment	5-1	33	CH0501.DOC	Word for Windows
Board of Directors Checklist	5-2	34	CH0502.DOC	Word for Windows
Board Composition Assessment Sheet	5-3	35	CH0503.DOC	Word for Windows
Sample Board Survey	5-4	36	CH0504.DOC	Word for Windows
Implementation Checklist	5-5	37	CH0505.DOC	Word for Windows

F. RESOURCES FOR FURTHER STUDY

Topic: Board of Directors

Publications and Periodicals

Note: There are dozens, if not hundreds of books on boards. Here are a few of particular benefit.

Nonprofit Board Answer Book: Practical Guidelines for Board Members and Chief Executives, by Robert C. Andringa and Ted Engstrom, National Center for Nonprofit Boards, ISBN 0925299804, 1997

Boards That Make a Difference: A New Design for Leadership in Nonprofit and Public Organizations, Second Edition, by John Carver, Jossey-Bass, ISBN 0-7879-0811-8, 1997

Secrets of Successful Boards, edited by Carol Weisman, Board Builders, ISBN 0966616812, 1998

The Board Member's Book: Making a Difference in Voluntary Organizations, by Brian O'Connell, The Foundation Center, New York

The Mission-Based Board Member, by Peter C. Brinckerhoff, 16-page booklet with all the board-related issues in *Mission-Based Management*—can be ordered at *www.missionbased.com*

Note: In the area of periodicals, there are a few good ones that either are dedicated completely to board issues, or have portions of each issue set aside for items of special interest to board members or staff who interact with governing volunteers.

Board and Administrator: Published monthly, offers good articles on how to run meetings, improve board/staff relationships, etc. by Aspen Publishers, (301) 417-7650

Board Member: Published monthly by the National Center for Nonprofit Boards (see website section below)

Chronicle of Philanthropy: Published every two weeks. Subscription also includes annual resource guide to the sector—worth the price of subscription itself. Call, or visit their website: *www.philanthropy.com*

Nonprofit Times: Visit their website: *www.nonprofittimes.com*

Nonprofit World: Published six times a year. Call, or visit their website: *http://danenet.wicip.org/snpo/NPWIndex/NPW.htm*

Software

Hmm. Board management software? Interesting idea. Haven't seen any yet, but a program to track board information—names, numbers, e-mail, preferences of committees, length of service, areas represented (locations, interests, ethnicities), family info, attendance, committees, etc. could have some real value. If you want to, this could be set up with a few hours work on any of the standard database programs. And you could *sell* it over the web as shareware, and become a social entrepreneur!

(continued)

Topic: Board of Directors *(continued)*

Websites

National Center for Nonprofit Boards: *www.ncnb.org*. NCNB is the place for board issues. They have great publications, do excellent training, and are a terrific resource for all things surrounding the board of directors. A membership in this organization is an excellent investment.

The Carver Governance Forum: *www.carvergovernance.com*

On-Line Courses

Learning Institute for Nonprofit Organizations: *www.uwex.edu/li*. The Learning Institute provides live satellite training in a variety of subjects, including boards of directors, strategic planning, fund-raising, marketing, social entrepreneurship, managing volunteers, etc. These courses are being put on the web as well.

6

Managing Your People

A. STRAIGHT FROM *MISSION-BASED MANAGEMENT*

Here are seven essential ingredients of being a mission-based manager. We start with these because if you don't face them head on now, your staff will beat you about the neck and shoulders with them later! Seriously, talk about these philosophies early, and then have discussions around which managers naturally evidence these tenets, and which will need coaching. For most organizations this is a major, long-term, behavioral change.

1. The Only Reason There Are Staff Is Because There Are People to Serve. The Only Reason There Are Managers Is Because the Staff Doing the Service Need Support.

The Executive Director is not the most important person in the not-for-profit. He or she may be the most *powerful*, but not the most important. If all staff realize that management exists to find and manage resources to allow line staff to do their jobs, then the priorities become much clearer, the roles begin to change a bit, and the organization starts to head in the correct direction.

2. Managers Are Enablers, Not "Restrictors."

Good management should be a supportive, assistive function rather than a harsh power game, telling people why they can't do things. As an enabler, your role is to support your staff in accomplishing the goals of the organization. This support means doing what it takes to get the job done. It includes fighting for resources for your staff, fixing things that aren't right, getting distractions large and small out of the way, and participating in budget and planning activities, no matter what your level in the organization. This fundamental principle allows you to see your job in very human terms. Your job as a supervisor is to take some of the load off the people you supervise and let them do their jobs.

3. The Supervisor/Supervised Relationship Is Two-Way.

The relationships you develop with your staff, like any other relationships, are two-way. That means that both the supervisor and the supervised have a responsibility to make things work. Additionally, if the closer you go toward the people you serve the more important people doing the service are, then the supervisor—instead of spending time restricting and controlling—should be facilitating getting resources to his or her employees. As we all know, relationships will not work if you always talk and never listen, if you only give ideas and are never receptive to those of your staff, or if you make all the decisions and don't delegate.

4. Treat Others the Way You Would Want to Be Treated.

Honesty, fairness, and consistency are the key characteristics of a successful manager. Honesty means not promising to do something you cannot deliver ("I'll get back to you on that tomorrow"); fairness means treating all of your staff equally (what goes for Sam has to go for Sally); and consistency means asking for rules to be followed and then enforcing them when you say you will. Say what you mean and mean what you say.

5. Be a Leader, but Willing to Follow.

This means that you are a leader who takes risks on behalf of your staff. It also means you let your staff take the lead when they are right. (This happens more than you or I want to admit.) It also means being very human and part of the team, so that you pitch in and do the most menial task when it is necessary to help support your staff.

6. If You Are Going to Help Your Staff, You Need to Keep in Touch.

Knowing what is going on with your line staff has never been more important. The further you are from line work, the more important it is. Make the time to work with line workers. My rule is one day per quarter at the very least, and more if the size and locations that you operate allow it. This task (which too many managers think is a waste of time) is, in truth, an essential component of the job.

7. Communication Is Not About What You Say. It's About What They Hear!

Consistent with the idea that the line staff are the most important in any organization is the concept that what really matters in communications is what is received, not what is sent. Thus you have to check to make sure that the information you transmit and/or receive is the information that was (respectively) received or transmitted. You can't assume—you have to check.

B. BASELINE SELF-ASSESSMENT

Form 6-1 Staff Management Self-Assessment		
Does the organization chart and culture place the people that the organization serves in the primary (top) position?	**3**	**–1**
Are staff who directly provide service included in budget development and other decisions?	**3**	**–1**
Do staff from all levels of the organization serve on most staff committees?	**2**	**0**
Are staff at all levels given the opportunity to review draft strategic plans, marketing plans, and monthly financials?	**4**	**–2**
Is a staff satisfaction survey completed at least every 18 months?	**3**	**–1**
Are exit interviews conducted for all voluntarily departing staff?	**3**	**0**
Are there at least two all-staff social events annually?	**3**	**0**
Are staff evaluations done at least annually?	**3**	**–2**
Are all staff provided training and/or continuing education at least 10 hours per year per person above any training needed for licensure or accreditation?	**3**	**0**
If staff training above licensure or accreditation is over 20 hours per year per person add this . . .	**5**	**0**
Are staff encouraged to innovate and take risks? Is there a component of the staff evaluation that includes rewarding innovation?	**2**	**0**
Do the staff formally evaluate their supervisors?	**2**	**–1**
Does staff have both responsibility and authority to meet service needs?	**3**	**–1**
Is there a staff recognition program? Was it designed by staff (not management)?	**1**	**–1**
Total of column score Add each column up and put the answer here ➔		
TOTAL SCORE Add total scores from Yes and No columns and put the answer here ➔		

● CH0601.DOC

SCORING ANALYSIS:

40–32 Excellent
31–21 Very Good
20–14 Adequate
Less than 14—You are not getting the benefit you should out of this resource.

You might give some thought to having this part of the self-assessment done by a larger staff group. See where they think you are at this point.

C. WORKSHEETS AND CHECKLISTS

Form 6-2 Training Checklist—Staff Management				
_____	**Training Type**	**For Which Staff**	**Deadline**	**Responsible Person**
	Communications	All		
	Supervision	All supervisors—annually		
	Customer Service	All staff—annually		
	Understanding Finances	All staff—12 sessions over 1 year		

 CH0602.DOC

Form 6-3 Checklist—Staff Management

___	Activity	Rationale	Deadline	Responsible Person
	Review evaluation process. Consider making it two-way. Add rewards for innovation. (See Form 6-4.)	Consistent with bottom-up management approach.		
	Develop/amend staff recognition program based on line staff input.	Consistent with bottom-up management approach.		
	If one has not been administered in the past 18 months, develop and administer a staff satisfaction survey.	Consistent with bottom-up management approach. The first line of defense against staff turnover, *if* you implement the ideas the survey gives you.		
	Develop two staff social events per year. Ask line staff for input on location, date, activities, etc.	Great opportunity for staff communication, learning about peers.		
	Review all staff training, and current budget allocation for training. Consider appointing key staff person to find training in house, on-line, or in our local community.	An essential part of both retaining staff, and remaining competitive.		
	Assure that staff from all levels of the organization sit on every staff committee. Provide any new members of the committees with orientation and background information.	Grows your internal stars, retains the best staff, and gives you perspectives on issues that you can't know.		
	Hold communications training annually for all staff.	*Essential*—1 to 2 hours per year.		
	Hold customer service training for all staff annually.	Ditto.		

● CH0603.DOC

The next four pages are a sample two-way evaluation that shows not only the kinds of questions to ask, but the process as well.

Form 6-4 Sample Two-Way Evaluation Form

DATE _____

Personnel Evaluation Form

NAME _____   SUPERVISOR _____

TITLE _____   EVALUATOR _____

WORK PERIOD COVERED BY THIS EVALUATION_____

NEXT EVALUATION DATE   DATE HIRED _____

The purpose of evaluations is to conduct a formal review of the employee's job performance and accomplishments, as well as the working relationship between the employee and his/her supervisor.

Both the employee and the supervisor take part in the evaluation by filling out these forms and reviewing them together.

STEP 1. Supervisor and Employee each fill our their forms. Supervisor fills out merit raise/bonus recommendation form and submits it to Financial Manager.

STEP 2. Supervisor and Employee exchange forms (not merit raise/bonus recommendations) and discuss evaluation.

STEP 3. Revisions are agreed to, submitted to Financial Manager for typing, signing, and filing.

STEP 4. Supervisor meets with President to discuss merit/bonus recommendation.

SUPERVISOR QUESTIONS REGARDING THE EMPLOYEE

I.   JOB PERFORMANCE
      A. How has the employee performed in terms of quality?

      B. Of quantity?

II.   ATTENDANCE, PUNCTUALITY—Is the employee on time, does he/she pay attention to breaks, lunch periods?

(continued)

Form 6-4 Sample Two-Way Evaluation Form *(continued)*

III.   ATTITUDE
    A.   Toward work?

    B.   Toward coworkers?

    C.   Toward supervisors?

    D.   Toward clients/vendors?

IV.   COMMUNICATIONS—How do you rate the employee's:
    A.   Listening skills: Does he/she listen and understand?

    B.   Speaking skills (internal—to other employees): Does he/she speak clearly and
        effectively?

    C.   Speaking skills—In public?

V.   CREATIVITY—What new ideas, processes, products, methods has the employee
    contributed to the firm?

VI.   GENERAL OBSERVATIONS ON THE EMPLOYEE

VII.   GOAL REVIEW
At the previous evaluation, the employee and supervisor set the following goals to be
accomplished by now. Were they accomplished?

           <u>GOAL</u>   <u>ACCOMPLISHED</u>

VIII.   GOALS FOR NEXT EVALUATION
Below the employee and the supervisor should write THREE or more goals to be
accomplished by the next evaluation.

(continued)

Form 6-4 Sample Two-Way Evaluation Form *(continued)*

EMPLOYEE QUESTIONS REGARDING THE SUPERVISOR

I. DELEGATION
    A. Are your job assignments clear and easy to follow?

    B. Are you delegated enough responsibility?

    C. Are you delegated the authority to complete your tasks?

II. COMMUNICATIONS
    A. Does the supervisor spend enough time with you?

    B. Does he/she speak clearly and effectively?

    C. Does he/she listen to you carefully?

III. DISCIPLINE—Has the supervisor's criticism of you been fair and explained fully?

IV. GOALS REVIEW
    At the previous evaluation, the employee and supervisor set the following goals to be accomplished by now. Were they accomplished?

<u>GOAL</u>   <u>ACCOMPLISHED</u>

We have read these evaluation forms and have discussed their contents together.

SIGNED _____   SIGNED _____
                    SUPERVISOR   EMPLOYEE

DATE _____   DATE _____

(continued)

Form 6-4 Sample Two-Way Evaluation Form (continued)

BONUS OR SALARY ADJUSTMENTS

DATE _____

EMPLOYEE NAME _____

EVALUATION DATE _____

EVALUATION BY _____

LAST SALARY INCREASE _____ $ _____ $ _____
                                  DATE   FROM   TO

LAST PERFORMANCE BONUS _____   AMOUNT $ _____

I recommend the following compensation:

  A. Salary Increase: _____ % FROM $_____ TO $_____

    Effective Date _____

  B. Bonus: $ _____

    To be paid as follows: _____

  C. Other _____

    _____

SIGNED _____
                      SUPERVISOR

****

I Agree _____ I Disagree _____

CHANGES _____

    _____

SIGNED _____
                  EXECUTIVE DIRECTOR

DATE _____

⬤ CH0604.DOC

Form 6-5 Implementation Checklist Topic: Staff Management		
Measurable Outcome	**Deadline**	**Person or Group Responsible**

D. ☞ HANDS-ON

☞ **HANDS-ON:** Try this exercise with your staff. At a staff meeting, read off the following list (exactly) without warning. Read it slowly and deliberately:

Bed, Rest, Slumber, Snooze, Pillow, Sheet, Nap, Mattress, Snore, Dream.

Now ask the staff to write down as many as they can remember. Give them a minute or two. Ask how many people got six words (ask them to raise hands). Some will have gotten six. Ask if anyone got eight. Compliment them. Ask who wrote down the word "Bed," the first word you read. About half will have. Compliment them. Ask everyone who wrote down "Dream," the last word you read. About the same number will have. Now, and this is the key, ask everyone who wrote down the word "Sleep" to raise their hands—and keep their hands up. If your group is like the dozens I've done this with, over half will have written down "Sleep," and *you never read it!* Have everyone look around to see how many hands were raised.

Make the point with your staff that the reason they wrote down "Sleep" was that they associated it with the rest of the words you read, but they felt so strongly that they heard it, that they *wrote it down.* Now, if you were to have gone back to them in a week and asked for notes on what you said, they would have "proof" (documentation) that you said "Sleep" because they wrote it down!

☞ **HANDS-ON:** Try this with your staff. Make a copy of the figure below. Hand it out at a staff meeting and tell people *exactly* the following:

"Take this, add one line, and turn this into a six."

IX

Give the staff a minute or two to get the right answer, and perhaps 1 in 10 will. The answer, by the way, is:

SIX

I used to use this exercise to teach people to learn how to solve problems in different ways. But, in 1988, my then six-year-old son Benjamin was talking to me as I was preparing for a presentation. He was asking the age-old question, "What do you do at work, Daddy?" and I was trying my best to explain the job of management consultant to not-for-profits in terms that he could understand. While talking, we came upon a copy of my training material that included the "IX" exercise. Aha! Here was a way that I could at least distract Benjamin from my inability to give him a satisfactory answer to my occupation. "Benjamin," I said, showing him the IX just as on the preceding page. "Take the pencil and with one line, turn this into a six." With no hesitation at all, he grabbed the pencil, added an "S" before the IX and said, "Like this?" I was floored. I mean, I knew he was smart (*my* child and all that egotistic drivel), but only about 10% of adults get this at all, much less immediately. What was going on?

What was going on, of course, was that Benjamin, as a first grader, had never learned about roman numerals. When he looked at a "IX," he saw an "icks," not a "nine," which is what adults see. In short, we, as adults have *too much information, too much education, too much knowledge* to solve this problem. Later that week, I was visiting Benjamin's classroom, and I asked the teacher if I could repeat the activity with the class. Of 30 kids in the room, all 30 got it immediately.

E. FORMS ON THE COMPANION CD-ROM

Form Name	Form #	Workbook Page	File Name	File Format
Staff Management Self-Assessment	6-1	44	CH0601.DOC	Word for Windows
Training Checklist—Staff Management	6-2	45	CH0602.DOC	Word for Windows
Checklist—Staff Management	6-3	46	CH0603.DOC	Word for Windows
Sample Two-Way Evaluation Form	6-4	47	CH0604.DOC	Word for Windows
Implementation Checklist	6-5	51	CH0605.DOC	Word for Windows

F. RESOURCES FOR FURTHER STUDY

Topic: Staff Management

Books

Human Resources Management for Public and Nonprofit Organizations, by Joan Pynes, Jossey-Bass, ISBN 0-7879-0808-8, 1997

Staff Screening Toolkit: Nonprofit Risk Management Center, ISBN 1-893210-00-6, 1998

Nonprofit Compensation and Benefits Practices, by Carol L. Barbieto and Jack P. Bowman, John Wiley & Sons, ISBN 0-471-18089-0, 1998

Nonprofit Compensation, Benefits, and Employment Law, by David G. Samuels and Howard Pianko, John Wiley & Sons, ISBN 0-471-19304-6, 1998

Software

There is a lot of HR software out there, but nothing I am aware of at this writing on staff management for not-for-profits.

Websites

Human Resources Links on the Web: *http://www.nbs.ntu.ac.uk/staff/lyerj/hrm_link.htm.* One word here: Wow!

The Nonprofit Manager's Toolkit: *www.benton.org/Practice/Toolkit/.* Another wow! Lots and lots of good ideas.

Staff Training and Development: *www.mapnp.org/library/trng_dev/trng_dev.htm.* More good stuff from Carter McNamara and the Free Management Site.

Overview of Supervision: *www.mapnp.org/library/suprvise/suprvise.htm.* Ditto.

On-Line Courses

Learning Institute for Nonprofit Organizations: *www.uwex.edu/li.* The Learning Institute provides live satellite training in a variety of subjects, including boards of directors, strategic planning, fund-raising, marketing, social entrepreneurship, managing volunteers, etc. These courses are being put on the web as well.

7

The Wired Not-For-Profit

A. STRAIGHT FROM *MISSION-BASED MANAGEMENT*

Here are four important ideas from Chapter 7 in *Mission-Based Management*. I cannot over-emphasize the importance of becoming and remaining technologically savvy. The ability to enhance your organization's capability to do good mission through good technology is virtually endless. You, or someone in your organization, must have the tech-smarts to handle rapid changes, making the best decisions on available hardware and software. But everyone has to understand these four key ideas, particularly your management team and your board.

1. The State-of-the-Art Hardware or Software You Just Bought Will Always Be Outdated in Under Ten Minutes.

The concept here is to move ahead, and use the tech you need now. Don't wait for the best, best, best stuff to come out. Top-of-the-line harddrives, chips, and video accessories cost the most, and will be out-gizmo'd in an hour anyway. Go for the level of quality just under the top, it will be much less expensive. For example, as this is written a one gigahertz chip is just being introduced. I'm telling all my clients to ask for 600 megahertz chips, since they are now not the new, new thing, and thus much more economical.

2. Just Because You Can't Keep Up with All the Changes, Doesn't Mean You Shouldn't Pay Attention to Them.

This is true not only in hardware, but in software. Subscribe to McAffee.com's annual service that includes an online assessment of available upgrades, patches, and improvements, usually at no cost. I usually recommend to my clients that they assess every major upgrade in key software, but skip one full version (that is, go from version 4.0 to version 6.0) to get the best value. Pay attention, and often improvements will make sense sooner rather than later.

3. The Cost-Benefit Ratio Is Rapidly Tipping to the Benefit Side, But Only for Flexible Organizations.

Tech is no longer a luxury. It is ubiquitous, part of everyday life. Many state, federal, and even foundation funders are requiring that their grantees have websites, and file forms and reports by e-mail or through other online methods. Certain accountability and outcome measures can only be provided through integrated technological solutions. Certainly communications, training, and access to a larger market is a result of the use of good technology. Tech is a tool. Get the tools you need to do your job. This does *not* mean that everyone in your organization needs a laptop, cell phone, and pager!

4. Tech Can Get in the Way of Providing Good Mission.

Like any other significant change, we can get so wrapped up in the wonders of technology that we lose sight of our mission. Personally, I feel that automated answering systems are very guilty of this, at least for human service organizations. Remember that technology is supposed to enhance your ability to provide mission, not detract from it. If you are constantly fighting tech bugs (often because you are trying to eke out one more year from antiquated hardware or software) you may be doing more harm than good.

B. BASELINE SELF-ASSESSMENT

Form 7-1 The Wired Not-for-Profit Self-Assessment	Yes	No
Do we consider technology an important investment?	3	−1
Does the organization have a website? Has it been updated in the past 30 days?	4	−3
On the website, is there a special section with targeted information for staff?	3	0
On the website is there a special section with targeted information for the board?	3	0
Does the organization use the e-mail in its communication with staff and volunteers?	3	0
Does the organization accept donations online?	2	−1
Does the organization have security systems in place to stop unauthorized access to its computers from inside and outside the organization?	3	−3
Do the appropriate staff have cell phones and beepers?	3	0
Are all sites of the organization networked (either hardwired or through an intra-net)?	4	−3
Does the organization do a quarterly (four times a year) technology assessment?	3	0
Does the organization have a single staff (or volunteer) who is primarily responsible for technological upkeep and updating?	2	−1
Do staff get access to classes in software and hardware use?	2	−2
Does the organization have e-mail for all staff?	3	0
Does the organization subscribe to one periodical that covers not-for-profit technological issues?	1	−1
Total of column score Add each column up and put the answer here ➜		
TOTAL SCORE Add total scores from Yes and No columns and put the answer here ➜		

● CH0701.DOC

SCORING ANALYSIS:

39–32 Excellent
31–23 Very Good
22–14 Adequate
Less than 14—You are not getting the benefit you should out of this resource.

Start with the technology you currently have in place. Focus on outcomes, not on bells and whistles. Are there free updates to your software? Do you need to start over in hardware? How can you get faster access to the net? You will find more things to do than you have funds to do them, so prioritize—and get some help. Take note of my Hands-On suggestion about National Honor Society high school students later in this chapter: They have to give community service. Go see the NHS advisor at your local high school(s) and ask if you can be the site for their most computer-savvy kids!

C. WORKSHEETS AND CHECKLISTS

Form 7-2 Training Checklist—Technology

____	Training Type	For Which Staff	Deadline	Responsible Person
	Software Use	Software users—quarterly		
	Technology Security	All—semi-annually		

● CH0702.DOC

Form 7-3 Checklist—Software

____	Action	Rationale	Deadline	Responsible Person
	Subscribe to McAffee.com and check all software for updates.	Checks for free updates, patches, etc. Also provides virus software for all computers.		
	Make master list of all software and versions.	Helps to assure that software is updated at reasonable intervals.		
	Check on sites like *www.download.com* and *www.davecentral.com.*	Checks for free utilities, demos of new software.		

● CH0703.DOC

Form 7-4 Checklist—Website

	Action	Rationale or Frequency	Deadline	Responsible Person
___	Make sure all links are active.	Quarterly check		
	Check ease of donations.	Quarterly check		
	Make sure all information is current.	Monthly check		
	Compress files for faster download.	Make all images compressed to speed download		
	Include secure sections for staff and board.	A great way to improve internal communications		

● CH0704.DOC

Form 7-5 Checklist—Hardware

___	Action	Rationale or Frequency	Deadline	Responsible Person
	Hire, or designate and train, a primary tech staff person.	You need a staff tech guru. Even if you only have five staff, one needs to be the primary tech person.		
	Have complete hardware review for potential upgrade needs.	Annually.		
	Form tech committee with our state or national trade association.	You learn from your peers, and don't reinvent the wheel.		
	Subscribe to a nonprofit tech journal.	Same as above.		
	Perform communications cost check for phones, pagers, laptops.	Annually—but check for cell phone rates quarterly.		

● CH0705.DOC

Form 7-6 Implementation Checklist Topic: Technology		
Measurable Outcome	**Deadline**	**Person or Group Responsible**

 CH0706.DOC

D. ☞ HANDS-ON

☞ **HANDS-ON:** You need a CIO (Chief Information Officer). Even if you can't afford to have someone full time in this role, you need to have someone in your organization who understands and likes technology, and who also understands what you do, how you do it, and why. This person's job will be to match up the mission with the technology to enhance and support it. In the words of a computer-savvy friend of mine, "you need to get a higher geek-quotient." I agree.

☞ **HANDS-ON:** Voice mail is great, but always have your phone answered during regular office hours by a real person and have your staff check their voice mail regularly.

☞ **HANDS-ON:** Your offices need access to the net. Now. But make sure that each physical office, home, place or worship, school, or other location only has one line to the net. If you have more than one computer at a site, network it, and use one server to access the outside world. It is more economical and easier to secure.

☞ **HANDS-ON:** Speaking of security, make sure you have up-to-date software called firewalls on all your computers that connect to the net. This is particularly important if you have 24-7 access through a cable modem or ISDN line. And assure that you have good virus protection. A great site for this is *www.mcaffee.com.*

☞ **HANDS-ON:** Make sure that at least one full backup a month gets off site: Take it home. If the computers don't break, but the building burns or floods, that off-site backup will save you. One of the cheapest ways to get this done is with a read/write CD recorder. They are relatively cheap as I write this, and the amount of data you can store is staggering. If you have really fast net access, through T-1, ISDN, or cable modems, you might do the backup on a remote server. Several net-based firms offer this service for really low prices. I use one to store some key files such as presentations or samples to access when I am on the road, in case I forget to bring them along. Again *www.mcaffee.com* offers this service, among many others.

☞ **HANDS-ON:** A caution here: In many cases general software like Excel or QuickBooks can be adapted to a wide variety of needs, and is much, much cheaper than the custom version. It may well be cheaper to send a staff person to a series of classes on the software (or buy a course on CD-ROM) than to buy custom or high-end software.

☞ **HANDS-ON:** You can get test or demo versions of most software free online. Locations like *www.downloads.com, www.shareware.com,* and even most starting portals like Yahoo! or Excite offer free downloadable software. If you go to a manufacturer's site, you can download test versions for free. But remember, most of this software stops working in 30 days, or the work you do can't be saved. So try it, see if you like it, but don't depend on it.

☞ **HANDS-ON:** On another note, there is lots of shareware on the net—and it is free, or very low cost, but you get what you pay for. For some small, focused applications, it is terrific, but for larger things like accounting, it rarely fills the bill. Go to *www.shareware.com* to check this out.

☞ **HANDS-ON:** Another techno-whiz caution: Don't assume that everyone needs every gadget—they probably don't. I saw a stunning piece of research recently that said fully 25% of people who wear pagers 24 hours a day are paged less than once per month! I know that "needing" a pager is a statement that you are important, and that many people do need them. The question is: Is it ego, or is it essential?

☞ **HANDS-ON:** Having discussed wiring, remember that wireless networks work well, and are much, much cheaper than rewiring a whole building. Some work through your electrical system, some are truly wireless. Check this option out before you hard wire!

☞ **HANDS-ON:** You want your website to provide a number of things:

1. More, much more, information than is possible in your printed materials. Don't just scan your brochures into the page. Offer more in-depth information, access to other sites that are concerned about the same issues, more detailed info about your hours, pictures of your staff, information on volunteering, etc. You have no limit on what you can put on the web.

2. A number of points of contact. A general e-mail link is essential, but also

have feedback loops that go to specific areas, such as intake, or fund-raising staff. And, of course, remember to include phone numbers, addresses, and names!

3. Specific areas for specific groups. For example, most of my web-savvy clients have parts of their site just for board members (with minutes of meetings, glossaries of jargon, contact points for other board members, etc.), others just for staff (who is new, whose birthday it is, minutes of all meetings, new forms, etc.) and for people concerned with the organization. There are literally limitless ways to use your website to build community support, and increase donations and volunteer time.

☞ **HANDS-ON:** If you don't have a managers' group on technology sponsored by your local United Way or your state trade association, get them to start one. There should be two types of groups, one for the Executive Directors, and one for the CIOs. Get together quarterly to talk about hardware, software, and all the applications of technology that are being used to do more mission.

☞ **HANDS-ON:** Don't forget your non-wired board members in a rush to tech-up. Board members should not be punished or treated like second-class citizens if they do not have access to a computer or have e-mail. This problem is rapidly waning in the United States, but will continue for some sectors for a long time. Be sensitive, and check it out!

☞ **HANDS-ON:** Popular word processing programs like WordPerfect and Word come with templates for newsletters, business cards, posters, and brochures already built in. Combine that with the wide array of newsletter, business card, poster, and brochure stock in various designs and colors at all the major office stores, and you have a recipe for quick, inexpensive, and professional-looking marketing materials made to order, *in small quantities,* on demand.

☞ **HANDS-ON:** Ok, so you aren't big enough to get a full-time CIO. I have a solution. Go back to high school. Seriously. High schools are full of bright, tech-savvy kids. In some school districts, they have to have a certain number of community service hours to graduate. In all school districts, the National Honor Society kids (the best and the brightest of any school) have to donate at least 50 hours of community service during their junior year and 10 more in their senior year. Go to the high school, talk to the NHS advisor, and get the tech kids to work at your organization!

E. FORMS ON THE COMPANION CD-ROM

Form Name	Form #	Workbook Page	File Name	File Format
The Wired Not-for-Profit Self-Assessment	7-1	57	CH0701.DOC	Word for Windows
Training Checklist—Technology	7-2	58	CH0702.DOC	Word for Windows
Checklist—Software	7-3	58	CH0703.DOC	Word for Windows
Checklist—Website	7-4	59	CH0704.DOC	Word for Windows
Checklist—Hardware	7-5	60	CH0705.DOC	Word for Windows
Implementation Checklist	7-6	61	CH0706.DOC	Word for Windows

F. RESOURCES FOR FURTHER STUDY

Topic: Technology

Books

The Nonprofit Internet Handbook, by Gary Grobman, White Hat Communications, ISBN 0-9653653-6-0, 1999

Selecting Computer Software, Accountants for the Public Interest—no ISBN available

Selecting Software for Non-Profit Organizations and Trade Associations, by Sheldon Needle, Computer Training Services, ISBN 0-917429-20-6, 1999

Software

Remember that the outcomes of the software are important, but so are ease of use and technical support! There is, of course, a ton of software for fund-raising, direct mail, donor-management, and the like. Not being a fund-raising consultant, I dare not give you any recommendations!

For a list (and some reviews) of specific nonprofit software, go to *www.npinfotech.org/ TNOPSI/index.htm.* This site reviews a huge number of software programs specifically designed for nonprofits.

For various targeted software, you can search at a number of websites, including *www.davecentral.com, www.andover.net,* and *www.cnet.com.*

Websites

Technology Tips for Nonprofit Organizations: *www.coyotecom.com/tips.html.* Lots of good stuff here.

All about Computers, Technology, and the Web: *www.mapnp.org/library/infomgmt/ infomgmt.htm.* More great information from the Free Management Site.

Art's technology toolkit for nonprofits: *www.nptoolkit.org/.* A great resource.

TechSoup: *www.techsoup.org/index.html.* An intersection of all things not-for-profit and technology.

Tech News For Human Services Organizations: *www.uwnyc.org/tech.htm.* Live from New York!

On-Line Courses

None that I know of at this writing, but by the time you read this, there probably will be five! Go to the broad-based websites noted in Chapter 3 and look for training online.

8

Creating the Social Entrepreneur

A. STRAIGHT FROM *MISSION-BASED MANAGEMENT*

Here are a few important ideas from *Mission-Based Management* on the subject of social entrepreneurism. Remember that your organization has to take risks to serve people at the highest level—innovation requires risk. And, to make the risk reasonable for your unique situation, business planning skills are the tool of choice. Don't think of business as a bad word. It can be a great resource.

1. Social Entrepreneurs Have These Characteristics.

They are willing to take reasonable risk on behalf of the people their organization serves.

They are constantly looking for new ways to serve their constituencies, and to add value to existing services.

They understand that all resource allocations are really stewardship investments.

They weigh the social and financial return of each of these investments.

They understand the difference between needs and wants.

They always keep mission first, but know that without money, there is no mission output.

2. Taking Risk Is an Inherently Good Thing. Taking Reasonable Risk Is Good Stewardship.

3. Making Risk Reasonable Is the Function of the Business Planning Process.

Risk is the engine of innovation. Innovation is crucial to keeping up with the rapidly changing wants and expectations of your many markets. So taking risk is a good thing, not a bad thing. But good stewardship requires that you make your risk taking reasonable in light of your financial condition, your markets, and your organizational culture. Thus the term "reasonable." How do you assure yourself that your risks are reasonable? By using the business planning cycle to assess risks thoroughly, and decide what risks are right for you now.

B. BASELINE SELF-ASSESSMENT

Form 8-1 Social Entrepreneurship Self-Assessment		
	Yes	**No**
Has the organization investigated (or is currently pursuing) non-traditional business activities to supplement income?	3	0
Does the organization weigh the mission return and the financial return of every investment (and view expenditures as investments?)	3	0
Have the staff and board identified the organization's core competencies?	3	–2
Is the organization constantly looking for ways to match these competencies with the markets' wants?	5	1
Does the organization have a list of criteria for new service ideas?	3	–1
Does the organization have a social entrepreneurship team?	3	0
Are program options or change opportunities free of restriction from facilities or debt you already have?	2	–2
Are the concerns of staff and service recipients acknowledged and addressed when change is initiated?	2	0
Are core values and the mission statement discussed when changes are considered?	2	–3
Have you discussed with board and staff the organizational willingness to take risk?	2	0
Is change initiated as an improvement without criticizing what has been done before?	1	0
Is innovation encouraged and are rewards provided at evaluation time?	2	0
Total of column score Add each column up and put the answer here ➔		
TOTAL SCORE Add total scores from Yes and No columns and put the answer here ➔		

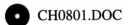 CH0801.DOC

SCORING ANALYSIS:

33–26 Excellent
25–20 Very Good
19–12 Adequate
Less than 12—You are not getting the benefit you should out of this resource.

In this chapter, I've provided you with a lot more hands-on materials to get started. But before you do, talk through the characteristics of social entrepreneurism with your key staff and board. Focus particularly on two things: The idea that risk is a good thing, and the concept of thinking of expenditures as investments. It is really important to have widespread acceptance of these two concepts if you are to become and remain entrepreneurial.

C. WORKSHEETS AND CHECKLISTS

Form 8-2 Training Checklist—Social Entrepreneurship				
___	**Training Type**	**For Which Staff**	**Deadline**	**Responsible Person**
	Business Planning	Your social entrepreneurship staff		
	Business Financing	CFO		
	Innovation and Internal Idea Generation	Any that want it		
	Social Entrepreneur Conferences	All SE team members		

● CH0802.DOC

Form 8-3 Social Entrepreneurship Readiness Checklist

Area	Readiness Item	Yes	No	Don't Know
Mission	Have the staff and board reviewed the idea of business development in relation to the organization's mission statement?			
	Are revisions or updates of the mission necessary?			
	Have you decided on the mission uses for the business and the mission uses for any profits?			
Risk	Have the board and staff discussed the risk inherent in new business development?			
	Have limits been set on venture capital to put at risk?			
	Do your board and staff view resource allocations as investments rather than expenditures?			
	Do your board and staff understand that the desired outcome for a not-for-profit business is a mix of mission return and financial return?			
Systems	Does the organization have personnel and finance policies that have been revised in the past 24 months?			
	Does the organization have a strategic plan that is current?			
	Does the organization have the information systems, payroll, accounts payable, and receivable systems that can accommodate growth?			
	Is the organization's financial accounting software able to track multiple projects and/or businesses?			
Skills	Are all of the following skills available within the staff and governing volunteers: planning, budgeting, pricing, marketing, project management?			
	Are skills and experience available within the industry or area that you have chosen to pursue?			
	Has the management team made the commitment to allow talented and experienced individuals to use their skills to develop the new business?			

(continued)

Form 8-3 Social Entrepreneurship Readiness Checklist *(continued)*				
Area	**Readiness Item**	**Yes**	**No**	**Don't Know**
Skills *(cont.)*	Have you generated a list of your organization's core competencies?			
Space	Is there readily available appropriate physical space to house the business?			
	Is there adequate equipment, wiring, plumbing, ventilation, security, and lighting for the business?			
Finance	Has the organization as a whole been profitable the past three years?			
	Does the organization have at least 90 days of cash or cash equivalents on hand?			
	Does the organization have an excellent relationship with its banker?			
	Does the organization have a line of credit?			
	Does the organization have a current ratio of 1.0 or higher?			
	Does the organization have a debt to net worth of .3 or less?			
	Will any of your funders penalize you for any net income from the business?			
TOTALS:	Add up the number of Yes, No, and Don't Know answers and put the total in the column to the right.			

● CH0803.DOC

There are twenty-four items to review in the list above. If more than eight answers are "No," I'd go back and take the time to improve your score. You need to have your organization in good shape to move ahead before you develop a new, and inevitably risky, venture.

On the following pages are forms and formats to help you develop an idea into a business plan.

Form 8-4 Business Idea Basics

On this form, fill in the information below as completely as you can.

Product or service description:

Market:

Your expertise in this business:

The mission outcome of the business:

How soon the business should start:

Your profit goal for the business (how much and by when):

CH0804.DOC

Form 8-5 Financial Basics

Item	Cost	Comments

Labor
    Fixed
    Variable		

Administration		
Rent		
Utilities		
Fringe benefits		
Travel		
Equipment		
Licenses		

Marketing
    Advertising
    Printing
    Web site
    Trade show		

Engineering		
Other Costs		

CH0805.DOC

Form 8-6 Pricing Basics		
Our pricing will be as follows:		
Number	**Unit Price**	**Comments**

⦿ CH0806.DOC

Now let's look at the steps of the process that you should have completed, and what this chapter will provide you. Form 8-7 shows you the outcomes you can expect by completing the materials provided here. Note that some parts of the plan will be completed after you finish using the information you honed here.

Form 8-7 Business Development Process Review			
Business Development Step	**Should Already Be Completed**	**Will Be Completed in This Chapter**	**Will Be Completed Later**
1. Review your mission statement	____		
2. Assess your willingness to take risk	____		
3. Decide on your mission outcomes from the business	____		
4. Generate your business ideas	____		
5. Develop preliminary feasibility studies	____		
6. Develop a final feasibility study	____Most Key Questions	____Some Final Numbers	
7. Develop a business plan		____ Most Key Decisions and Financials	____ Full Written Draft
8. Implement the plan			____

⦿ CH0807.DOC

For the remaining sections read each part of the explanatory materials, and fill in the forms as best you can. I suggest doing all your work *in pencil*, as you will almost certainly come back and revise things as you move through the forms.

1. Product/service description

What product(s) or service(s) will your new venture or expansion provide? How tightly can you define them? "We will do education" is not a good service definition. Your research in the preliminary feasibility study should have focused you on a more specific definition.

❏ **EXAMPLE:** *"We will provide legal-aid services to citizens of two new counties."*

❏ **EXAMPLE:** *"We will assist seniors in improving their nutrition by personal counseling in senior centers."*

❏ **EXAMPLE:** *"We will provide testing for children from birth to 3 years old for long-term physical disabilities in coordination with our county medical society."*

Write a definition of your product(s) or service(s) below:

_____

_____

_____

_____

2. Definition of the market

Now that you have defined your product or service, you need to focus on who you will work for, your market. Who are those people? Where are they? How many of them are there? All of these questions should have been already discussed. Again you want to be as specific as you can.

❏ **EXAMPLE:** *"Our market for legal aid will be citizens making under $20,000 per year."*

❏ **EXAMPLE:** *"Our market for seniors will be residents of senior housing within 20 miles of our office."*

Who will your market be? Write it below:

_____

_____

_____

_____

3. Definition of the target market(s)

Now you need to increase the focus on the market, by targeting a particular segment for your highest research, sales, and customer service efforts. Who will that be for you? Think through a smaller component of the market you listed above that makes the most business sense for you to target. That target should be the best match between your core competencies and the wants of the market.

❑ **EXAMPLE:** *"Our target market for legal aid will be people in need of primary legal services. Our secondary market will be seniors in need of legal consumer assistance."*

❑ **EXAMPLE:** *"Our target market for nutrition services will be those seniors referred to us by their physicians. Our secondary market will be other seniors who attend our free educational sessions."*

List the target market for your business below. If you have identified a secondary market focus, list that as well.

_____

_____

_____

_____

4. Listing of five core wants of the target market(s)

The next step is to identify the five core wants of your target markets. Once you have done this, you may find that you cannot meet those wants, and have to return to a review, and possible revision, of your target markets.

What is it that your markets want? Remember, the issue is *wants* not *needs!* How do you know that these are the markets' wants? Did you ask them, or are you making (perhaps dangerous) assumptions?

Some examples of wants might be: flexible hours, lowest possible price, personal treatment, or state-of-the-art services.

List the five core wants of your markets on the lines below.

1. _____

2. _____

3. _____

4. _____

5. _____

5. Listing of core competencies

You now have your target markets' wants in hand. How will you meet them? Do you have the core competencies that match up with your markets' wants? Let's see . . .

Market Want: _____ Our Core Competence: _____

Market Want: _____ Our Core Competence: _____

Market Want: _____ Our Core Competence: _____

Market Want: _____ Our Core Competence: _____

Market Want: _____ Our Core Competence: _____

Do your competencies match up well to meet the wants of the target markets? If not, you may want to go back to step 4 and change your target market, or you may need to find ways to strengthen or acquire certain competencies.

6. Reaching the markets

How will you establish relations with your market(s)? This includes not just sales, but doing regular customer research, developing long-term relationships and, of course, promotion and sales. What tactics will you use? If you are entering a new market, how will you establish a beachhead?

Examples could include trade show presentations, cold calls, referrals, advertising, or some other outreach function.

List how you plan to reach out to, and stay in touch with, your markets:

_____

_____

_____

_____

7. The mission outcomes of the business

This is a crucial step. Now that you have defined your business, what will the mission outcome of the business be? Some specific mission service? Profit to do more direct mission? A combination?

List your expectations below, in as specific a manner as possible.

_____

_____

_____

_____

Key Financials

Let's start with a quick review of the terminology and what you need to accomplish on these forms.

1. Start-up costs

How much are you putting at risk? What costs will be incurred before your business opens, after it opens, and during the remaining start-up period? Where will this money come from? See Form 8-8.

2. Initial size of the business

What is your initial size going to be in terms of units of production, revenue, employees, and space? All businesses have a size below which it doesn't make sense to operate. On the other hand, you can have starting goals that are too high for you to afford in working capital, sales staff, production capacity, or administrative support. You should complete Form 8-9 on initial size and then review the implications of that size in terms of market demand, production capacity, personnel, and finance. If any of these four areas conflict with your initial assessment, now is an excellent time to revise your starting size.

3. Fixed costs

Once you know the starting size, you can fill in your fixed costs form. Remember, fixed costs are the costs that don't change when sales go up (or down). Rent, utilities, depreciation, insurance, and administrative overhead are examples of fixed costs. You were asked to do an initial examination of your fixed costs before you started. Take those numbers and apply them to your initial size of your business by filling out Form 8-10.

4. Variable costs

Variable costs refer to costs that change with sales volume. Direct labor, raw materials, waste, shipping, and consumable supplies are all examples of variable costs. Your job is to list all of your variable costs for each unit of sale on Form 8-11. The key here is to be as precise and detailed as possible.

Form 8-8 Start-up Cost Estimation

Cost Item	Cost Estimate
Wages	
Benefits	
Training	
Rent	
Utilities	
Equipment (Detail)	
Supplies	
Licenses	
Marketing (Detail)	
Printing	
Travel	
Raw Materials	
Engineering	
Legal	
Accounting	
TOTAL START-UP COSTS:	

CH0808.DOC

Form 8-9 Initial Size of Business			
	Year One	**Year Two**	**Year Three**
Sales (in units of sale)			
Sales (in dollars)			

Rationale: *The reason we think we need to be this size to start.*

Checklist: *Will our market support this size? Can we produce this much product or service? Can we do it with a high level of quality and customer satisfaction?*

NOTES:

 CH0809.DOC

Form 8-10 Fixed Costs Estimation

Fixed Cost Item	Cost Estimation Per Year		
	Year 1	Year 2	Year 3
Wages			
Fringes			
Rent			
Utilities			
Depreciation			
Marketing			
Legal			
Printing			
Travel			
Administration			
TOTAL FIXED COSTS PER YEAR:			

NOTES:

● CH0810.DOC

Form 8-11 Variable Cost Estimation

Variable Cost Item	Cost Estimate Per Item
Direct Labor	
Direct Fringes	
Raw Materials	
Supplies	
Direct Travel	
Direct Utilities	
Direct Shipping	
Waste	
Direct Phone	
Total Variable Cost Per Item:	

NOTES:

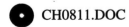 CH0811.DOC

5. Volume projections

On the volume projection form (Form 8-12) list the number of units of service you expect to provide per month for the first year and per quarter for the next two. Remember that being overly optimistic *or* pessimistic here will hurt your ability to price accurately and, more importantly, competitively. If you are planning to sell more than one service, use the multiple forms provided. This form has the most benefit if you are charging per unit of service.

Form 8-12 Volume Projection

First Item Volume Projection:

Month	1	2	3	4	5	6	7	8	9	10	11	12
Sales Units Year 1												

Quarter	First			Second			Third			Fourth		
Year 2												
Year 3												

Second Item Volume Projection:

Month	1	2	3	4	5	6	7	8	9	10	11	12
Sales Units Year 1												

Quarter	First			Second			Third			Fourth		
Year 2												
Year 3												

Third Item Volume Projection:

Month	1	2	3	4	5	6	7	8	9	10	11	12
Sales Units Year 1												

Quarter	First			Second			Third			Fourth		
Year 2												
Year 3												

Fourth Item Volume Projection:

Month	1	2	3	4	5	6	7	8	9	10	11	12
Sales Units Year 1												

Quarter	First			Second			Third			Fourth		
Year 2												
Year 3												

● CH0812.DOC

6. Cash flow projections

Form 8-13 will take a bit of time and attention. You can do it by hand, on the form below, or adapt it to a spreadsheet, if you brought a laptop.

Remember, cash is different than income and expense. On this form, you want to include all of your receipts and all of your disbursements in the month (or quarter) where they actually are received or disbursed. Depreciation is not a cash expense. Debt service (including interest and principal) is. Loans that you receive should be included in your receipts.

You will note that the form includes your start-up costs, and initial start-up capital. You should be able to retrieve the costs from your start-up cost form that you filled out earlier.

Enter the information, then do the addition and subtraction. If you are doing this by hand, *do it in pencil!* It is almost certain that you will revise this form.

Are there months where you run out of cash? Are there months where your cash is critically low? If so, you may need to go back and revise the amount of cash you need to start with. Don't forget to take into account the amount of time your customer will take to pay you after you deliver the product or service. A sale in April, for example, may not result in cash in your checking account until June.

Form 8-13 Cash Flow Projection Form

YOUR BUSINESS
PRO FORMA CASH FLOW ANALYSIS

YEAR ONE

Month	1	2	3	4	5	6	7	8	9	10	11	12	TTL
UNITS OF SALE PER MONTH													
CASH RECEIPTS													

DISBURSEMENTS

	1	2	3	4	5	6	7	8	9	10	11	12	TTL
Variable Labor													
Variable Payroll/Fringe													
Supplies													
Advertising													
Vehicle Operation													
Repairs													
Insurance													
Legal & Accounting													
Salaries													
Loan													
Telephone													
Rent/Utilities													

	1	2	3	4	5	6	7	8	9	10	11	12	TTL
TOTAL DISBURSEMENTS													

	1	2	3	4	5	6	7	8	9	10	11	12	TTL
NET CASH FLOW													
CUMULATIVE CASH FLOW													

	1	2	3	4	5	6	7	8	9	10	11	12	TTL
STARTING CASH ON HAND													
CASH RECEIPTS													
CASH DISBURSEMENTS													
ENDING CASH ON HAND													

 CH0813.XLS

7. Pricing—single item

If your business is going to start with just one product or service, this section is for you. If you have more than one, go directly to section 8, which follows.

As you build your price, remember, it is composed of four parts: fixed costs, variable costs, profit, and market forces. The first three raise the price, the fourth holds it down or even reduces it. Also remember that the amount of fixed costs that you allocate to each unit of sale is dependent on how many sales you expect each year. If your sales projections turn out to have been unreasonably optimistic, you will not have recovered all your fixed costs. If they wind up having been too low, you may well have had to price higher than you should have in a highly competitive marketplace. So be careful.

But, do seek to add all of your costs in the price, and to add a profit! If the price you decide upon is different than what you started with earlier in this chapter, you may need to revise your cash flows!

Form 8-14 Pricing Chart		
Item	**Cost**	**Instructions**
Fixed Costs Per Year		
Units of Sales Per Year		
Fixed Cost Per Unit		Divide the fixed costs per year by the units of sales per year to arrive at fixed cost per unit.
Variable Cost Per Unit		
Profit Per Unit		
Total Price Per Unit		Add up the per unit costs to get the total price per unit.

 CH0814.DOC

8. Pricing—multiple services

The issues in pricing many services, or an array of services, are similar to a single item, but they have one crucial issue that is different: the spread of your fixed costs. Look at the example below, and then fill in the form for your own array of products or services. Form 8-15 is designed for a maximum of four products or services. If you have more, just draw up a similar form with more columns.

Remember, the core components of price remain the same: fixed costs, variable costs, profit, and the market. I've included an example (Form 8-16) to help you with this important form.

Form 8-15 Multiple Service Pricing

Total Fixed Costs Per Year for the Business: _____

	Service 1	Service 2	Service 3	Service 4
Fixed Cost % Allocation				
Fixed Costs				
Units of Sale				
Fixed Cost Per Unit				
Variable Cost Per Unit				
Profit Per Unit				
Price Per Unit				

 CH0815.DOC

Form 8-16 Example of Multiple Service Pricing

Total Fixed Costs Per Year for the Business: $100,000

	Item 1	Item 2	Item 3	Item 4
Fixed Cost % Allocation	20%	15%	40%	25%
Fixed Costs	$20,000	$15,000	$40,000	$25,000
Units of Sale	10,000	16,500	27,500	12,000
Fixed Cost Per Unit	$2.00	$ .91	$1.45	$2.08
Variable Cost Per Unit	$ .21	$ .11	$ .45	$ .17
Profit Per Unit	$ .05	$ .10	$ .17	$ .22
Price Per Unit	$2.26	$1.12	$2.07	$2.47

CH0816.DOC

9. Breakeven

Now you are ready for a heads-up check on your work to this point: a breakeven analysis. The formula on the next page will allow you to calculate breakeven for one product or for multiple products. Breakeven analysis is designed to show you how many units of sale you need to recover all your costs at a certain mix of costs and price. If you find that your cost/price mix takes too long to recover, you may need to move your price up (if the market will bear that) or move your costs down (if you can). Understanding breakeven is important to ongoing business operations as well. It will allow you to quickly assess the impact of discounting or price cutting to retain business.

Variable Cost Per Unit: _____

Price Per Unit: _____

Fixed Cost Per Year: _____

$$\text{Breakeven} = \frac{\text{Fixed Cost}}{(\text{Price} - \text{Variable Cost})}$$

Calculate the breakeven now for your product. Can you provide that much service, or manufacture that much product? How soon? Will the market bear this amount of sales?

10. Income and expense projections

Now we need to start our income and expense sheets. Don't despair—much of the information is already gathered.

Use Form 8-17 to enter your data for your first year of business by month and then for the next two years by quarter. Complete the first year, and then work your way by quarters in the latter forms.

Remember that this should be an accrual form. Put the income in when it is earned, and the same for expenses. Enter interest only, with no repayment of debt principal, and depreciation instead of capital purchases.

Form 8-17 Income and Expense Projection

YOUR BUSINESS

PRO FORMA PROFIT AND LOSS STATEMENT

YEAR ONE

Month	1	2	3	4	5	6	7	8	9	10	11	12	Total
GROSS SALES													
OPERATING EXPENSES													
Salaries													
Variable Labor													
Fringe Benefits & Payroll Taxes													
Materials & Supplies													
Telephone													
Legal/Accounting													
Advertising													
Rent/Utilities													
Depreciation													
Insurance													
Licenses													
Repairs													
Vehicle Operation & Maintenance													
Interest													
TTL OPER EXPENSES													
PROFIT (LOSS)													
EARNINGS TO DATE													

CH0817.XLS

11. *Working capital needs*

Working capital is the money you need to operate your business between the time you provide a service or deliver a product and the time you receive payment. The larger your business and/or the longer your customers take to pay you, the more working capital you require. As your business grows, you will need more cash in working capital. Where will it come from? Form 8-18 and your cash flow projections will tell you.

Form 8-18 Working Capital		
Working Capital Needs—Year One		
Item	**Item Need**	**Total Needs**
Projected Income		
Days To Payment		
Total Working Capital Needed (Income X—Days To Payment/365)	(Copy Sum ➜)	
Additional Cash Needs—Year One		
Equipment Purchases		
Minus Loans	( )	
Start-up Costs		
Total Additional Cash Needs	(Copy Sum ➜)	
Total Cash Needed—Year One		

● CH0818.DOC

Note that in year two and three, you compute working capital needed by replacing total sales with the difference (growth) in sales from years one and two. All other calculations remain the same.

D. BUSINESS PLANNING SEQUENCE

Now, at last, you are ready to plan. On the following pages, list the sequence of events that must occur for your business to become a reality. Add some tentative dates, and who you will assign to complete the task. Do this list in pencil, as it is almost certain to change. Think through all the things that have to happen, and list them here.

Example:

Task To Be Completed	Deadline	Person Assigned
1. Talk to banker about loan	8/1	Mike
2. Estimate debt from cash flow	7/15	Eric
3. Talk to board members about risk	7/1	Sally

With this list, which was written down as people thought about things, the writer would first need to revise and put things in order. Then from this list, develop goals for your business. The idea of the sequence list is to get all the activities down in front of you. This will enable you to gather the work into goals and objectives.

Remember: A *goal* is a statement of desired outcome. It may or may not be quantified or have a deadline. An *objective* has to include four things:

1. Support of the goal
2. A quantified outcome
3. A deadline
4. A person responsible for its achievement

The example of activities included above might turn into the goal and objectives below.

Goal One: Obtain adequate financing for business.			
Objective	**Deadline**	**Costs**	**Person Responsible**
1. Estimate total debt needs for project	7/1	Staff time (10 hours)	Eric
2. Meet with board to discuss acceptable risk	7/15	Staff and board time (1 hour)	Sally and Eric
3. Meet with banker	7/20	Staff time (2 hours)	Eric and Mike
4. Develop loan application	7/30	Staff time (8 hours)	Eric and Mike
5. Present loan application	8/15	Staff time (1 hour)	Eric and Mike

Add as many of the following as you can: objectives, costs, assigned personnel.

Form 8-19 Tasks To Be Completed			
	Tasks To Be Completed	Deadline	Person Assigned
1			
2			
3			
4			
5			
6			
7			
8			
9			
10			
11			
12			
13			
14			
15			
16			
17			
18			
19			
20			
21			
22			
23			
24			

CH0819.DOC

Goal One:

Objective	Deadline	Costs	Person Responsible
1.			
2.			
3.			
4.			
5.			

Notes on Goal One:

Goal Two:

Objective	Deadline	Costs	Person Responsible
1.			
2.			
3.			
4.			
5.			

Notes on Goal Two:

Goal Three:			
Objective	Deadline	Costs	Person Responsible
1.			
2.			
3.			
4.			
5.			

Notes on Goal Three:

Goal Four:			
Objective	Deadline	Costs	Person Responsible
1.			
2.			
3.			
4.			
5.			

Notes on Goal Four:

Goal Five:

Objective	Deadline	Costs	Person Responsible
1.			
2.			
3.			
4.			
5.			

Notes on Goal Five:

Goal Six:

Objective	Deadline	Costs	Person Responsible
1.			
2.			
3.			
4.			
5.			

Notes on Goal Six:

Goal Seven:			
Objective	**Deadline**	**Costs**	**Person Responsible**
1.			
2.			
3.			
4.			
5.			

Notes on Goal Seven:

Goal Eight:			
Objective	**Deadline**	**Costs**	**Person Responsible**
1.			
2.			
3.			
4.			
5.			

Notes on Goal Eight:

Goal Nine:

Objective	Deadline	Costs	Person Responsible
1.			
2.			
3.			
4.			
5.			

Notes on Goal Nine:

Goal Ten:

Objective	Deadline	Costs	Person Responsible
1.			
2.			
3.			
4.			
5.			

Notes on Goal Ten:

Form 8-20 Checklist—Business Planning

	Action	For Which Staff	Deadline	Responsible Person
___	Review mission statement	Senior staff and board		
	Internal risk analysis	Senior staff and board		
	Selection of business mission outcomes	All staff		
	Idea generation			
	Development of business criteria			

● CH0820.DOC

Form 8-21 Implementation Checklist		Topic: Social Entrepreneurship
Measurable Outcome	**Deadline**	**Person or Group Responsible**

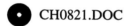 CH0821.DOC

E. ☞ HANDS-ON

☞ **HANDS-ON:** You need a lot of business ideas when you begin, and your staff is a great resource for you. Get your staff together for a brainstorming session with a facilitator. Explain the need for a business and the social outcome that the business will meet. Then ask for ideas (remember in brainstorming every idea is a good one). In a minute or two the ideas will start to flow. If there are problems in getting the group started, use the questions below.

1. What is your organization's primary purpose as a not-for-profit organization?
2. What are your organization's core competencies?
3. What are the markets (the groups of people) you want to target?
4. What do these markets really want?
5. How do those wants match up with your competencies?

When you have your list, develop some criteria against which to weigh each idea. For example, you might want to prioritize businesses that can be started up in less than six months, with no more than $10,000 invested and have a direct social impact. The combination of criteria will be up to you, but by establishing what is important now, you can fairly weigh all your potential business ideas, and not upset the people whose ideas are not followed up.

E. FORMS ON THE COMPANION CD-ROM

Form Name	Form #	Workbook Page	File Name	File Format
Social Entrepreneurship Self-Assessment	8-1	67	CH0801.DOC	Word for Windows
Training Checklist—Social Entrepreneurship	8-2	68	CH0802.DOC	Word for Windows
Social Entrepreneurship Readiness Checklist	8-3	69	CH0803.DOC	Word for Windows
Business Idea Basics	8-4	71	CH0804.DOC	Word for Windows
Financial Basics	8-5	72	CH0805.DOC	Word for Windows
Pricing Basics	8-6	73	CH0806.DOC	Word for Windows
Business Development Process Review	8-7	73	CH0807.DOC	Word for Windows
Start-up Cost Estimation	8-8	78	CH0808.DOC	Word for Windows
Initial Size of Business	8-9	79	CH0809.DOC	Word for Windows
Fixed Cost Estimation	8-10	80	CH0810.DOC	Word for Windows
Variable Cost Estimation	8-11	81	CH0811.DOC	Word for Windows
Volume Projection	8-12	82	CH0812.DOC	Word for Windows
Cash Flow Projection Form	8-13	84	CH0813.XLS	Excel

(continued)

Form Name	Form #	Workbook Page	File Name	File Format
Pricing Chart	8-14	85	CH0814.DOC	Word for Windows
Multiple Pricing Items	8-15	86	CH0815.DOC	Word for Windows
Example of Multiple-Service Pricing	8-16	86	CH0816.DOC	Word for Windows
Income and Expense Projections	8-17	88	CH0817.XLS	Excel
Working Capital	8-18	89	CH0818.DOC	Word for Windows
Tasks To Be Completed	8-19	91	CH0819.DOC	Word for Windows
Checklist—Business Planning	8-20	97	CH0820.DOC	Word for Windows
Implementation Checklist	8-21	98	CH0821.DOC	Word for Windows

F. RESOURCES FOR FURTHER STUDY

Topic: Social Entrepreneurship

Books

Social Entrepreneurship, by Peter Brinckerhoff, John Wiley & Sons, ISBN 0-471-36282-4, 2000

Sustaining Innovation: Creating Nonprofits and Government Organizations That Innovate Naturally, by Paul Light, Jossey-Bass, ISBN 0-7879-4098-4, 1998

Enterprise in the Nonprofit Sector, by James Crimmins, The Rockefeller Fund, 0941182037 1994

Nonprofit Piggy Goes to Market, by Richard Steckel, Children's Museum of Denver, 1982

Managing the Double Bottom Line, by Sutia Kim Alter, Save the Children Federation, 2000

A Reader in Social Enterprise, edited by Kelvin Sealey, Pearson Custom Publishers, ISBN 0-536-60860-1, 2000

Software

Palo Alto Software's Business Plan Pro has gotten raves from many of my clients. I've tested it and like it, too. You can download a trial version at *www.paloalto.com.*

Websites

CEO Express: *www.ceoexpress.com.* This site provides you with quick access to marketing information, business planning tools, financing, and company research.

Sample Business Plans: *www.bplans.com/samples/index.cfm?affiliate=bplans.* This resource is too cool to miss. Full plans of dozens of different start-ups. Provided by Palo Alto Software.

IOMA Business: *www.ioma.com.* All sorts of business resources.

Social Entrepreneurship: *www.mapnp.org/library/soc_entr/soc_entr.htm.* Part of Carter McNamara's huge Free Management Site. A great resource.

Roberts Development Fund: *www.redf.org/.* A foundation that is on the cutting edge of social entrepreneurial issues.

On-Line Courses

None that I know of at this writing, but by the time you read this, there probably will be five! Go to the broadbased websites noted in Chapter 3 and look for training online.

9

Developing a Bias for Marketing

This is a crucial chapter to work on as a team. If everyone in the organization does not realize that they are crucial to the marketing of the organization, your mission output is doomed.

A. STRAIGHT FROM *MISSION-BASED MANAGEMENT*

Marketing is so, so important, and here are five crucial marketing concepts from *Mission-Based Management* to get you started on this vital part of your organization update. This material is so important that it would behoove you to integrate your marketing committee (both board and staff) into these discussions. Go over the five ideas below, and then do the self-assessment as a larger group.

1. Everything Everyone in Your Organization Does Every Day Is Marketing.

There is nowhere to hide from this concept. Every staff member and volunteer contributes (or detracts) from your organization's image in the community. Marketing is a team sport, and everyone is always playing. Remind your staff that, when they are very happy (or very unhappy) with a retail transaction, they are nearly always very happy (or very unhappy) with the actions of one of the lowest paid workers, not with the CEO, or Director of Marketing.

2. It's All About Wants, Not About Needs.

In the not-for-profit sector, we constantly pat ourselves on the back, because we fill needs in the community. While this is fine, we must also remember that in order to get people what they *need*, we have to give it to them in a way that they *want* it. All of us have needs. All of us seek wants. Don't confuse the two.

3. Ask, Ask, Ask, and Then Listen!

To find out what people want, you have to ask, and ask regularly. The biggest mistake people make in marketing (other than confusing needs and wants) is saying: "I've been in this field for 20 years, and I know what people want." Here is the truth: No one knows what anyone wants unless he or she has asked, and asked recently. People are fickle, and their wants are constantly changing. Ask, and then make sure you listen to what they want!

4. Customers Never Have Problems, Customers Only Have Crises.

We need to look at things through our customers' eyes, and have a sense of urgency about what we do for them. Remember the cardiologist's reminder to his staff: "What we do every day is a once in a lifetime experience for our patients. We need to never forget that." Good advice. Empower your staff to act, act with compassion and expertise, and act quickly. In our part of the world, nearly all the people who come through our doors have problems of one kind or another. Even if we see 10,000 similar people every year, each of them deserves to be treated as an individual, with a sensitivity to their urgent needs and wants.

5. With Price, the Issue Is Never Cost. It Is Always About Value!

If the issue was only price, we wouldn't have Rolls Royce automobiles, first-class airline seats, or Ritz-Carlton hotels. No one would pay $50 for a regular season baseball game ticket, or spend $5,000 at an auction for used (also known as antique) furniture. But they (and we) do. Why? Because we value the product or service enough. Put another way, we get what we want. What value does your organization provide to your clients, funders, staff, and volunteers? Is the value seen as that by your customers? Remember value is always from the perspective of the customer!

B. BASELINE SELF-ASSESSMENT

Form 9-1 Marketing Self-Assessment		
	Yes	**No**
Have you identified your organizational target markets for finders, people to serve, and referrers?	3	–3
Have all your staff had customer satisfaction training in the past year?	2	–1
Have you asked your target markets what they want, or how satisfied they are with your services in the past 24 months?	3	–1
Do you follow how many of your target markets return for more services?	3	–1
Do you have an organizational website?	5	–3
Does your website have separate areas for your different target markets?	3	–1
Has your website been reviewed and updated within the past 60 days?	3	–1
Does your website provide more information than your written materials?	3	–3
Do you have an organizational domain name?	2	–1
Are your marketing materials targeted to individual markets?	2	–1
Have your marketing materials been updated in the past 18 months?	1	–1
Do you empower your staff members to fix customers' problems promptly?	2	–2
Are you constantly trying to improve your services from your customers' point of view?	2	0
Do you track your key competitors?	2	0
Have you identified your organizational core competencies?	3	–2
Have you matched those competencies to your target markets' wants?	4	–2
Do you have a current marketing plan?	2	0
Are there specific marketing goals in your strategic plan?	2	0
Total of column score Add each column up and put the answer here ➜		
TOTAL SCORE Add total scores from Yes and No columns and put the answer here ➜		

⬤ CH0901.DOC

SCORING ANALYSIS:

47–39 Excellent
38–27 Very Good
26–14 Adequate
Less than 14—You are not getting the benefit you should out of this resource.

As you start working your way through marketing improvements, pick two things—your most important service (the one that does the most mission) and your fund-raising efforts. I suggest these two because the first does lots of mission and may or may not make money, while the second does no mission, and thus should make a ton of money. Who are your target markets in each area? What do they want? Are your marketing materials targeted to their wants?

C. WORKSHEETS AND CHECKLISTS

Form 9-2 Training Checklist—Marketing				
____	**Training Type**	**For Which Staff**	**Deadline**	**Responsible Person**
	The marketing team	All staff annually		
	Core competencies	Marketing team		
	Pricing	All financial and sales staff		
	Better surveys	Marketing team		
	Customer satisfaction	All staff annually		

● CH0902.DOC

Form 9-3 Marketing Checklist—Target Market Identification

—	Activity	Rationale	Deadline	Responsible Person
	Identify all discrete markets: internal, payor, service, and referral	This takes a while, you will be surprised how many you have.		
	Draft initial target markets	Using the large list, use your best guesses to pick an initial list of target markets.		
	Identify target market wants	Ask—and then use the next worksheet.		
	Identify internal core competencies	What do you *really* do *really* well?		
	Match core competencies with target market wants	Match one with the other-focusing on what you can do well that people want now. Or, do you need to ramp up your skills to meet a target market's wants?		
	Revise target market list as needed	You may find out that your target group should be another one.		

● CH0903.DOC

Form 9-4 What Do Your Markets Really Want?

CATEGORY	MARKET	WANTS As you identify your markets, ask them what they want, and put the information here. Then match up wants with core competencies in the next chart. Note that your markets can have more than one important want.		
Internal	Board			
	Staff			
	Other volunteers			
Payor				
Service				
Referral				

CH0904.DOC

Form 9-5 Our Core Competencies—Matching Up to Wants

For this form, fill in your organizational core competencies remembering to only put the things down that you are really, really good at. Then, fill in your top target markets, their wants, and see if your competencies match up. If they don't, you either need to ramp up your competencies, or change your target markets!

Our organizational core competencies are:

1		
2		
3		
4		
5		
6		

	Target Market	The Market Want	Our Competency
1			
2			
3			
4			
5			

● CH0905.DOC

Form 9-6 Marketing Checklist—Asking Informally

	Activity	Rationale	Deadline	Responsible Person
——	Train all staff in how to ask regularly about customer satisfaction. Focus on sales, reception, and marketing team first, then all staff.	You need to become a culture of asking.		
	Develop feedback loop to get information to marketing team.	The information does no good if it doesn't get to the right people.		
	Empower staff to fix identified problems.	If you ask, people will point out ways to improve. Most issues can and should be resolved quickly.		

● CH0906.DOC

Form 9-7 Marketing Checklist—Asking Surveys

――	Activity	Rationale	Deadline	Responsible Person
	List the markets you want to survey, and how often.	Asking on a regular, standardized basis is the only way to get defendable data that you can compare over time.		
	List what you want to know—but stay focused.	Remember you only have four minutes to survey, if you want people to respond!		
	Get some outside help to put the questions in the correct order and wording.	This is the time to get some expertise.		
	Put instructions on the front and end of the survey.	Tell people (briefly) why you are asking, when the deadline is, where to send the completed survey, and how to fill it out. And, say thank you!		
	Close the loop.	After you analyze the data, get back to the people you surveyed and tell them what you learned—it will increase your response rate next time.		
	Share the information internally.	You asked. You learned. Now, to improve you have to let people know what you found out—the good news and the bad news.		

● CH0907.DOC

Form 9-8 is a survey that was used by an East Coast rehabilitation center to assess their clients' satisfaction with their services. It was administered by interview in the client's home, so that the survey could be longer than usual.

Note that the numbers to the left of each question's answers are there to facilitate data entry. This was essentially a closed-choice survey. As you read it you will see that in some cases there is a mixed choice for identifying the respondents because in some cases the person with the disability was the respondent and, in some cases, it was the person's advocate.

Also note that this survey does not have (nor does it need) instructions in the beginning and at the end of the survey because the survey was administered by interview. If you send out surveys by mail, you *need* the instructions.

Form 9-8 Survey Sample

Date _____

Client name _____

Parent/guardian name _____

Client's age _____

1. Who is responding to this questionnaire? (Please circle the number.)
    4 Consumer
    3 Family member
    2 Guardian
    1 Advocate
    0 Other: _____

2. Sex of respondent:
    2 Female
    1 Male

3. Indicate this person's primary disability.
    5 Mental retardation
    4 Cerebral palsy
    3 Epilepsy
    2 Autism
    1 Other: _____
    0 Don't know

4. Where does this person live?
    6 Residential facility   Please describe: _____
    5 Parent's home
    4 Guardian's home
    3 Conservator's home
    2 On his/her own (with residential support)
    1 On his/her own (no support)
    0 Other

5. Do you know what The Center is?
    2 Yes
    1 No
    0 Not sure

6. When did you/_____ (insert name of client) first come in contact with The Center?
    5 Less than 6 months
    4 6 months to 2 years
    3 2 to 5 years
    2 5 to 10 years
    1 More than 10 years
    0 Don't know

7. Do you know your client program coordinator's name?
    2 Yes
    1 No
    0 Don't know

(continued)

Form 9-8 Survey Sample *(continued)*

8. How well did your coordinator explain your/_____'s rights and the services available to you?
    4 Explained very well
    3 Explained somewhat
    2 Not well explained
    1 Not explained at all
    0 Don't know

9. How satisfied are you with the assessment and the services that were recommended for you/_____?
    5 Very satisfied
    4 Somewhat satisfied

10. Do you feel your coordinator is acting on your/_____'s behalf in obtaining services for you?
    4 Yes, very much
    3 Yes, somewhat
    2 No, not very much
    1 No, not at all
    0 Not sure

11. What services are you/is _____ receiving as a result of The Center's assessment and referrals?

    _____

    _____

12. What providers are currently bringing these services to you/_____?

    _____

    _____

13. Does The Center contact you regularly to discuss your/_____'s progress?
    3 Yes
    2 No
    1 Sometimes
    0 Don't know

14. Have you contacted The Center about any questions or problems you have had?
    2 Yes
    1 No
    0 Don't know/Don't remember

15. If Yes, how helpful was the coordinator in solving your problems?
    5 Very helpful
    4 Somewhat helpful
    3 Not very helpful
    2 Not helpful at all
    1 I have not contacted The Center concerning a problem
    0 Don't know/Don't remember

(continued)

Form 9-8   Survey Sample *(continued)*

16. When you call The Center with a problem or question, how soon does the client program coordinator respond?
    5   Within 24 hours
    4   Within 1 week
    3   Within 2 weeks
    2   More than 2 weeks
    1   I have not contacted The Center concerning a problem
    0   Don't know

17. Did you feel this action was fast enough to address your situation?
    3   No
    2   Yes
    1   I have not contacted The Center concerning a problem
    0   Don't know

18. Are you satisfied with the amount of time your case manager spends with you/_____?
    5   Very satisfied
    4   Somewhat satisfied
    3   Neutral/It's OK
    2   Somewhat dissatisfied
    1   Very dissatisfied
    0   Not sure

19. Have you/has _____ received the assistance you hoped for since you/he/she began working with The Center?
    4   Yes, definitely
    3   Probably
    2   Probably not
    1   Definitely not
    0   Not sure

20. Would you refer another person with a disability to The Center?
    2   Yes
    1   No
    0   Don't know

21. What three things do you think The Center does best?

    _____

    _____

    _____

22. What three things do you think The Center could do better?

    _____

    _____

    _____

● CH0908.DOC

Form 9-9 Marketing Checklist—Asking Focus Groups

	Activity	Rationale	Deadline	Responsible Person
___	Choose the target markets you will want to focus on.	Pick carefully, as focus groups are great, but expensive.		
	Pick homogeneous groups to participate.	Don't mix people staff and funders, or business people and clients, for example.		
	Get a facilitator.	You need an outsider for these sessions.		
	Hold the session in a safe, neutral location.	Sounds obvious, but people regularly forget this.		
	Have the facilitator ask your questions in a priority order.	Ask your most important question third.		
	Audio tape the session, but don't videotape it.	You need the record, but the camera really inhibits many people.		

CH0909.DOC

Form 9-10 Marketing Checklist—Innovation/Value

____	Activity	Rationale	Deadline	Responsible Person
	Talk to staff regularly about risk taking—as a good thing.	Constant coaching on this is crucial, particularly when you are trying to overcome organizational inertia.		
	Role model this by trying new ideas, changing routines.	Walk the talk.		
	Focus on improving customer service 1% every day.	It's the small things that add up. Big changes often result in big resistance.		
	Add innovation to your employee evaluation materials.	Reward the behaviors you want to see.		
	Hold regular staff meetings whose sole topic is ways to improve services, even in the smallest ways.	This shows the issue is a priority.		

● CH0910.DOC

Form 9-11 Marketing Checklist—Marketing Materials

Check and see that your marketing materials have the characteristics that are checked—and don't have the characteristics with the X's. If there are things that need to be fixed, put it on the form.

____ Good Characteristic	What Needs to Be Fixed	Deadline	Responsible Person
____ Your mission statement			
____ Focus on one issue or market			
____ Brevity			
____ Connecting problems and solutions			
____ Professional appearance			
____ A source for more information (a name, phone number and e-mail)			
✗ Bad Characteristic	What Needs to Be Fixed	Deadline	Responsible Person
✗ Jargon (can high school students understand every word?)			
✗ Inappropriate photos (old, ones that you don't have releases for?)			
✗ Lack of focus (blah, blah, blah)			
✗ Asking for money (except in a fund-raising piece)			
✗ Out of date (do you mention Y2K, the Bicentennial, or going into the new millennium?)			
✗ Boring—again, ask your high schoolers			

⬤ CH0911.DOC

Form 9-12 Marketing Checklist—Website				
——	**Activity**	**Rationale**	**Deadline**	**Responsible Person**
	Do you have a website?	Welcome to the 21st century.		
	Does it include information that is in more depth?	There is no point in just reprinting your printed materials electronically. A website is an incredible resource— that takes work. You can't just set it and forget it.		
	Does it allow for people to contact you electronically—and does someone check their e-mail?	You want every available way for people to get in touch and find out more.		
	Can people make donations online?	A must.		
	Is the website checked for accuracy and currency every two weeks?	Things go out of date very fast.		
	Do you regularly (monthly) check other peer websites for good ideas?	Don't reinvent the wheel, and be aware of what your competition is doing.		

● CH0912.DOC

Form 9-13 Marketing Checklist—Competition

___	Activity	Rationale	Deadline	Responsible Person
	Do you have a current list of all your competition?	Why not?		
	Do you visit their facilities (and their websites) regularly?	A website is a great way to quietly keep track of what is going on.		
	Do you know why people use them?	Ask your network. They know.		
	Do you know their prices, and what services they provide?	You have to know this.		

● CH0913.DOC

Form 9-14 Implementation Checklist   Topic: Marketing

Measurable Outcome	Deadline	Person or Group Responsible

● CH0914.DOC

D. HANDS-ON

There is only one ☞ HANDS-ON in Chapter 9, and it recommends using one of the preceding forms.

E. FORMS ON THE COMPANION CD-ROM

Form Name	Form #	Workbook Page	File Name	File Format
Marketing Self-Assessment	9-1	104	CH0901.DOC	Word for Windows
Training Checklist— Marketing	9-2	105	CH0902.DOC	Word for Windows
Marketing Checklist— Target Market Identification	9-3	106	CH0903.DOC	Word for Windows
What Do Your Markets Really Want?	9-4	107	CH0904.DOC	Word for Windows
Our Core Competencies— Matching Up to Wants	9-5	108	CH0905.DOC	Word for Windows
Marketing Checklist— Asking Informally	9-6	109	CH0906.DOC	Word for Windows
Marketing Checklist— Asking Surveys	9-7	110	CH0907.DOC	Word for Windows
Survey Sample	9-8	112	CH0908.DOC	Word for Windows
Marketing Checklist— Asking Focus Groups	9-9	115	CH0909.DOC	Word for Windows
Marketing Checklist— Innovation/Value	9-10	116	CH0910.DOC	Word for Windows
Marketing Checklist— Marketing Materials	9-11	117	CH0911.DOC	Word for Windows
Marketing Checklist— Website	9-12	118	CH0912.DOC	Word for Windows
Marketing Checklist— Competition	9-13	119	CH0913.DOC	Word for Windows
Implementation Checklist	9-14	119	CH0914.DOC	Word for Windows

F. RESOURCES FOR FURTHER STUDY

Topic: Marketing

Books

Mission-Based Marketing, by Peter Brinckerhoff, John Wiley & Sons, ISBN 0-471-29693-7, 1996

Marketing Strategies for Nonprofit Organizations, by Siri Espy, Lyceum Books, ISBN 0-925085, 1995

Marketing Nonprofit Programs and Services, by Douglas Herron, Jossey-Bass, ISBN 0-7879-0326-4, 1996

Focus Groups: A Practical Guide for Applied Research, by Richard Krueger, Sage Press, ISBN 0-761-92070-6, 1994

Focus Groups: A Step-by-Step Guide, by Gloria Bader and Catherine Rossi, The Bader Group, ISBN 0-966-47080-X, 1998

Organizational Surveys: Tools for Assessment and Change, by Allen I. Kraut, Jossey-Bass, ISBN 0787-90234-9, 1996

Software

Again, there are a lot of pieces of software, but nearly all are tied to fund-raising marketing.

Websites

Sample Marketing Plans: *www.bplans.com/marketingplans/index.cfm?affiliate=bplans.* The corollary site to the business plan site noted in Chapter 8. Sample plans and even a marketing plan wizard.

Nonprofit Marketing FAQ: *www.leetassociates.com/faq1482/faq.htm.* A commercial site, but a good FAQ.

Profitable Public Relations for Non-Profit Marketing: *www.chevron.com/community/other/pub-relations/index.html.* Some good PR information, and some sample press releases.

The Nonprofit Marketing Library: *www.mapnp.org/library/mrktng/mrktng.htm.* Part of Carter McNamara's huge nonprofit resource directory.

On-Line Courses

Learning Institute for Nonprofit Organizations: *www.uwex.edu/li.* The Learning Institute provides live satellite training in a variety of subjects, including boards of directors, strategic planning, fund-raising, marketing, outcome measurement, social entrepreneurship, managing volunteers, etc. These courses are being put on the web as well.

10

Financial Empowerment

A. STRAIGHT FROM *MISSION-BASED MANAGEMENT*

When you deal with finances, you are often working with the most complex group of people—money people and mission people. As with the marketing assignment, you need to include your finance committee in your work on this chapter. You will get more out of the effort if you do. Start with the five core philosophies below, and listen carefully to the discussion. If you get agreement, you are on your way! If not, you will need to work through the barriers before you proceed.

1. No Money, No Mission.

This is, as you know, the second rule of not-for-profits, coming close (very close) after the first rule, "Mission, mission, and more mission!" Although many of us would like to live in a world where money and/or possessions were meaningless, we're stuck in this one, where money buys the things (people, buildings, equipment, food, supplies, transportation) that we need to do our mission. Part of our jobs as stewards is to make the most out of all of our resources, but this doesn't mean squandering them. Having money to do mission is a good thing. Having money in reserve to do mission later is a good thing, too. Mission rules, but money enables.

2. The More Everyone Knows About Your Financial Situation the Better— As Long As They Are Well Trained.

Don't hoard your information. Share it. As I said earlier, one of my favorite sayings is from John Chambers of Cisco, "No one of us is as smart as all of us." Share your financial and non-financial data with your staff after they are well trained in how to read it, and you will get a lot more out of your staff, they will better understand how the organization runs, and you will have more ownership throughout the organization.

3. Get People the Financial Information They Need, in the Format They Need It, in Time for Them to Use It Well.

With today's tech, you can get what people need to know to them in a format that they can understand, in a time frame where it is valuable. And, that doesn't always mean *more* information. For some volunteers it may even mean less, as long as that is more understandable. More on this a bit later.

4. The Budget Is a Contract.

Whether it is the overall budget (contract between staff and board) or a division budget (contract between executive director and division manager), your budgets should be looked at as contracts. In contracts, when people keep their promises, and live up to the provisions of the contract, they are left alone. Same here. If the staff keeps income and expenses within the contract (the budget) they should not be nitpicked at the board meetings. Same for that division manager. I'll show you a format in a few pages that will allow your board (and you) to do this kind of contract-based management.

5. Expenditures Are Investments.

We've already touched on this in Chapter 8 on social entrepreneurship. Remember that you are looking for two returns on your investments of people, equipment, property, and cash: Return on investment financially, and return on investment in mission. Some services are mission rich, and thus can be cash poor. A soup kitchen is a great example of this—you give away food, make no money, but do a tremendous amount of mission. Or, you may have a service that does very little (or no) mission, and thus should absolutely make money. An example of this would be fund-raising: No mission here, so it better post a profit! Another part of thinking of expenditures as investments is that you need to look at your options. Ask: "Is this the best place to invest this cash (or people, property, equipment) or is there a better place?" Remember, a steward's job is to get the *most* mission out of available resources, not just to spend it where it has always been spent. Situations change. Should your investments?

B. BASELINE SELF-ASSESSMENT

Form 10-1 Financial Empowerment Self-Assessment	Yes	No
Do you have at least 30 days cash on hand?	2	0
At least 60 days?	3	0
At least 90 days?	3	0
Has your organization been profitable in the past three years?	3	0
Do you have financial policies that have been updated in the past 18 months?	2	–3
Do you know which of your programs make money and which lose money?	4	–2
Do you have an endowment?	1	0
Do you get 5% of your income from earnings on your endowment?	4	0
Do you have and distribute a mission reserve chosen by line staff?	3	–1
Do you consider debt as an option to get a new service up and running?	1	0
Do you and your board view your expenditures as investments?	2	0
Do you involve staff in budget development?	1	–1
Do you involve staff in budget implementation?	2	–1
Do you share your financial information widely inside the organization?	2	–1
Do you have a banker with whom you meet regularly?	1	0
Do you have a line of credit?	2	0
Total of column score Add each column up and put the answer here ➔		
TOTAL SCORE Add total scores from Yes and No columns and put the answer here ➔		

● CH1001.DOC

SCORING ANALYSIS:

36–31 Excellent
30–23 Very Good
22–14 Adequate
Less than 14—You are not getting the benefit you should out of this resource.

Ok, so there is one set of assessment forms, but financial issues are so crucial (remember the second rule) that I have included two more forms which work together. These are great discussion tools for your board and staff, as they look at financial issues through both management policies and actual numbers.

The Financial Self-Assessment Tool is comprised of two forms. The first (Form 10-2) is called Financial Status. By completing this form, you will examine your overall financial status. To fill this in you will need your most recent income and expense statement, your most recent balance sheet, and your last audit. Simply fill in the form according to the instructions and do the simple arithmetic calculations. At the bottom of the form is a self-scoring grid that will allow you to look at how your organization measures up on this quick overview.

Form 10-2 Financial Status Self-Assessment Form

Indicator	Instructions	Point Calculation	Score
1. Did the organization have a positive net revenue • Last month? • Last fiscal year? • The previous fiscal year?	Look at your income and expenses. If revenues exceeded expenses, you had a positive net revenue.	For profits • Last month: 2 points • Last year: 3 points • Previous fiscal year: 2 points BONUS—if all were yes, add 3 points	
2. Liquidity (current ratio)	On your most recent balance sheet, take your current assets and divide them by your current liabilities.	• 1.5 to 2.5 gets 3 points • 1.0 to 1.49 gets 2 points • .75 to .99 gets 1 point • over 2.5 gets 1 point • under .75 gets 0 points	
3. Debt to net worth	From your balance sheet add up all your debt. Divide this number by your net worth (total assets minus total liabilities).	• .1 to .24 gets 1 point • .25 to .4 gets 3 points • .41 to .8 gets 2 points • .81 to 1.0 gets 1 point • over 1.0 gets 0 points • under .1 gets 0 points	
4. Fixed asset component	Take your total net fixed assets (minus depreciation) and divide them by total assets.	• up to .5 gets 3 points • .51 to .6 gets 2 points • .61 to .75 gets 1 point • over .76 gets 0 points	
5. Receivables component	Divide your receivables by your total assets. Compare this to the past six months' balance sheets.	• For a percentage that has grown or shrunk more than 15%— 0 points • For a percentage that has stayed ± 15 points—2 points	
6. Payables component	Divide your payables by your total liabilities. Compare to the last six months.	• For a percentage that has grown or shrunk more than 15%— 0 points • For a percentage that has stayed ± 15 points—2 points	

● CH1002.DOC

SCORING (Total for the scores for numbers 1–6):

19–17—You are in good initial shape.
16–14—Not bad, but can use some work.
13–10—You can get a lot more out of this area.
9–4—You need help now!

The second form (Form 10-3) is called the Management Status Self-Assessment Form. It looks at your internal controls and uses of your financial reporting. Again, fill in the form and review your score against the scoring chart.

Form 10-3 Management Status Self-Assessment Form

Indicator	Instructions	Point Calculation	Scoring
1. Reporting	Look at your financial reports. Examine who gets which reports. For example, does the senior management team get the same monthly income and expense report as the board?	• If everyone gets the same monthly report: 0 points • If *all* staff see monthly figures: 3 points • If monthly reports show actual, budget, and the difference for each line item: 3 points • If staff see their division's own income and expense statement monthly: 2 points	
2. Controls	Get out your financial policies.	• If your financial policies have been reviewed in the past 24 months: 2 points	
3. Budgeting	Think through your budgeting process.	• If only the CEO does the budgeting: −3 points • If senior managers develop their budgets: 1 point • If the Finance Committee reviews the budget prior to the board seeing it: 2 points • If all staff are involved in the budget development process: 4 points	
4. Pricing	Think through your pricing process.	• If your prices are reviewed at least quarterly: 2 points • If you have a fixed allocation for administration: −1 point	
5. Monitoring	Go to your financial policies and reporting.	• If you calculate financial ratios each month: 2 points • If you share those ratios with senior managers and the board finance committee: 1 point • If you have benchmarks or goals for the ratios: 2 points	
6. Checks and Balances	Go to your financial policies.	• If the board (or board representative) must approve taking on any debt, including borrowing on the line of credit: 2 points • If you have a two-signature requirement for amounts greater than 1% of your budget: 2 points • If you have a two signature requirement for checks less than 1% of your total budget: −1 point	

● CH1003.DOC

SCORING ANALYSIS:

31–25—You are in good initial shape.
24–20—Not bad, but can use some work.
19–10—You can get a lot more out of this area.
9–2—You need help now!

C. WORKSHEETS AND CHECKLISTS

Now that you are all self-assessed, let's look at some forms, formats, checklists, and other things that can help you. First the forms and formats. You need to put all of your reports in context. You need to make them easy to read, so that staff and volunteers can use them, perform their oversight function, and then move on, assuming you are still within your contract!

Form 10-4 is a sample income and expense statement. Note the columns that allow the reader to see what actually happened in the reporting period (usually a month) versus what the budget was (the context) and then what the difference was in both dollars and percentages. Then, the entire exercise is repeated for the year to date, to further put the information in useful form. Form 10-5 is a blank form for you to start with. Note: The blank forms are included on the CD-ROM as Excel files for you to use with your own data.

Form 10-4 Income and Expense Reporting Sample

LINE ITEM	MONTHLY ACTUAL	MONTHLY BUDGET	MONTHLY VARIANCE	% OF BUDGET	YTD ACTUAL	YTD BUDGET	YTD VARIANCE	% OF BUDGET
INCOME								
State Program	55,400	53,000	2,400	4.5%	310,045	321,000	(10,955)	–3.4%
Medicaid	65,443	61,000	4,443	7.3%	422,449	415,000	7,449	1.8%
United Way	5,000	10,000	(5,000)	–50.0%	30,000	60,000	(30,000)	–50.0%
Fees	18,440	19,500	(1,060)	–5.4%	114,598	124,600	(10,002)	–8.0%
TOTAL INCOME	144,533	144,000	533	0.4%	887,592	923,600	(36,008)	–3.9%
EXPENSES								
Salaries	105,800	107,900	(2,100)	–1.9%	623,980	602,300	21,680	3.6%
Fringes	9,522	9,711	(189)	–1.9%	56,158	54,207	1,951	3.6%
Occupancy	2,500	2,500	0	0.0%	15,000	15,000	0	0.0%
Insurance	8,000	8,000	0	0.0%	8,000	8,000	0	0.0%
Utilities	1,244	1,200	44	3.7%	7,698	7,400	298	4.0%
Telephone	867	900	(33)	–3.7%	4,680	5,400	(720)	–13.3%
Depreciation	6,588	6,588	0	0.0%	39,528	39,528	0	0.0%
Supplies	2,240	2,500	(260)	–10.4%	12,679	15,000	(2,321)	–15.5%
Travel	1,243	1,500	(257)	–17.1%	11,340	9,000	2,340	26.0%
TOTAL EXPENSE	138,004	140,799	(2,795)	–2.0%	779,063	755,835	23,228	3.1%
NET	$6,529	$3,201	$3,328	2.36%	$108,529	$167,765	($12,780)	–7.62%

CH1004.XLS

Form 10-5 Blank Income and Expense Form

YOUR BUSINESS
PRO FORMA PROFIT AND LOSS STATEMENT

YEAR ONE

Month	1	2	3	4	5	6	7	8	9	10	11	12	Total
GROSS SALES													
OPERATING EXPENSES													
Salaries													
Variable Labor													
Fringe Benefits & Payroll Taxes													
Materials & Supplies													
Telephone													
Legal/Accounting													
Advertising													
Rent/Utilities													
Depreciation													
Insurance													
Licenses													
Repairs													
Vehicle Operation & Maintenance													
Interest													
TOTAL OPERATING EXPENSES													
PROFIT (LOSS)													
EARNINGS TO DATE													

CH1005.XLS

Next is cash flow projection. In Forms 10-6 and 10-7 you see a sample projection for the next six months on cash in and cash out, as well as a blank form for you to start with. Remember, this is cash. No depreciation is included, but all debt services, equipment purchases, and loans received are.

Form 10-6 Cash Flow Projection Sample

Receipts	Month 1	Month 2	Month 3	Month 4	Month 5	Month 6
State Program	53,000	53,000	53,000	53,000	53,000	53,000
Medicaid	61,000	61,000	61,000	0	0	183,000
United Way	10,000	10,000	10,000	10,000	10,000	10,000
Fees	19,500	19,500	24,500	18,500	17,450	19,500
Debt Received	0	0	0	40,000	40,000	0
Donations	500	650	900	12,580	125	125
Total Receipts	**144,000**	**144,150**	**149,400**	**134,080**	**120,575**	**265,625**
Disbursements						
Salaries	107,900	107,900	107,900	107,900	107,900	107,900
Fringes	9,711	9,711	9,711	9,711	9,711	9,711
Occupancy	2,500	2,500	2,500	2,500	2,500	2,500
Insurance	0	0	0	48,000	0	0
Utilities	1,200	800	850	950	1,450	1,650
Telephone	900	900	900	900	900	900
Debt Service Paid	7,960	7,960	7,960	7,960	7,960	88,000
Supplies	2,500	2,500	2,500	2,500	2,500	2,500
Travel	600	560	2,540	120	450	3,450
Total Disbursements:	**133,271**	**132,831**	**134,861**	**180,541**	**133,371**	**216,611**
Starting Cash	**23,560**					
Net Cash Flow:	**10,729**	**11,319**	**14,539**	**(46,461)**	**(12,796)**	**49,014**
Ending Cash Bal.	**34,289**	**45,608**	**60,147**	**13,686**	**890**	**49,904**

 CH1006.XLS

Form 10-7 Blank Cash Flow Projection Form

YOUR BUSINESS

PRO FORMA CASH FLOW ANALYSIS   YEAR ONE

Month	1	2	3	4	5	6	7	8	9	10	11	12	TOTAL
UNITS OF SALE PER MONTH													
CASH RECEIPTS													
DISBURSEMENTS													
Variable Labor													
Variable Payroll/Fringe													
Supplies													
Advertising													
Vehicle Operation													
Repairs													
Insurance													
Legal & Accounting													
Salaries													
Loan													
Telephone													
Rent/Utilities													
TOTAL DISBURSEMENTS													
NET CASH FLOW													
CUMULATIVE CASH FLOW													
STARTING CASH ON HAND													
CASH RECEIPTS													
CASH DISBURSEMENTS													
ENDING CASH ON HAND													

CH1007.XLS

Form 10-8 Training Checklist—Financial Empowerment

——	Training Type	For Which Staff	Deadline	Responsible Person

● CH1008.DOC

Form 10-9 Estimating the Cash Needs of Growth

Programs	Start-up Costs	Current Budget	Next Yr. Budget	Days Payable This Yr.	Days Payable Next Yr.	CASH NEEDED
Existing Programs	0					
	0					
	0					
	0					
Total Existing Programs	0					
New Programs						
	0					
						Grand Total

Calculations for growth:

Step 1: Subtract "Next Yr" from "Current" budget
Step 2: Divide by 365
Step 3: Multiply by days payable

Calculations for increase in days payable:

Step 1: Subtract Days Payable this year from Days Payable next year
Step 2: Divide Next yr budget by 365
Step 3: Multiply by the days difference

● CH1009.XLS

You also need to be working with your banker on how much cash you will need for capital items, such as roofs, vans, computers, HVAC, and the like. This template will help you get started on that.

Form 10-10 Capital Planning Template						
Item	**Est. Cost**	**FY**	**FY**	**FY**	**FY**	**FY**
Buildings						
Machinery						
Vehicles						
Repairs						
Equipment						
Other						
TOTALS						

● CH1010.DOC

Let's now look at the information that you should be seeing at the staff and/or board level. At some point, in some form, at some level of detail, you should see the following:

1. Cash Flow Projection

While all of the other information listed below is important, you need to think of cash as your organization's blood: without it you die, and quickly. Even with the critical importance of cash, most organizations don't have a report that tells their staff or volunteers what their cash status will be in a few weeks or months. Does your organization have a cash flow projection? If not, you need one, and soon. You already have the information and experience to be able to develop one. I'll show you a sample of a cash flow projection later in the chapter that looks out six months, my recommended minimum.

2. Income and Expense

This report is basically a diary of what happened in your organization during the last reporting period, usually a month. You should see one of these monthly for the organization as a whole, and for any programs that you are particularly interested in or responsible for.

3. Balance Sheet

A balance sheet is another report you should get monthly, and it is closely linked to your income and expense statement. Your balance sheet is a financial snapshot of your organization, and it shows your assets, liabilities, and net worth. Most boards and staff use a balance sheet as the basis for management ratios, preferring the more understandable ratios to the somewhat esoteric balance sheet.

4. Payables

These are the things your organization owes others. As you look at the balance sheet, the question is: Are our payables growing while revenue is level? (This could mean you are running out of cash.) Are your payables shrinking rapidly? (This could indicate that your bills are being paid too promptly, which could cause a cash shortage.)

5. Receivables

These are the things people owe your organization. You will also find these on the balance sheet, and questions similar to those asked about payables should be answered. Are the receivables growing faster than income? If so, it may indicate that no one is paying attention to collections, or that the quality of what you are doing is slipping. Are receivables dropping rapidly? That could mean that you won't have much actual cash income in future months.

6. Non-Financial Indicators

In addition to the indicators of financial well-being that I have listed above, there are always some other non-financial indicators that you should look at regularly that can immediately have an impact on your finances. For example, occupancy, new members, staff turnover, patient days, attendance at worship services or in Sunday school, number of repeat customers are all numbers that, while not being counted in currency, do have an impact on your finances. Which indicators are best for you will depend on your organization, but find them, and then set a benchmark against which to monitor them.

Remember to show each and every one of these reports *in context*. Without context, the information loses value, and reading it becomes a fruitless expenditure of time. But no matter how your report, remember to see the crucial information, cast off the unimportant data, and focus on setting goals and budgets, and then monitor how your organization is performing.

Since one of my key concepts from *Mission-Based Management* was the idea of getting people the information they need, in a way that they can use it, when they need it, I've included a sample questionnaire for you to give to your staff and board to find out what they want.

Form 10-11 Financial Reporting Questionnaire

Questionnaire for Staff and Board	Financial Reporting

This questionnaire is intended to help us get the right information to our staff and board. We realize that some people probably get too much information, and some not enough. Thus, we have listed a number of reports, and ask you to fill in what you would like to see, how often you would like to see them, and whether you want a detailed report, or a summary report. There is also space for you to ask for information that is not listed. Thanks for your input.

Please fill this out and return to _____ by _____

Name: _____ Date: _____

Report or Display	I do not need to see this	I need this report	Check how you would like the report			
			Summary	Detail	Monthly	Quarterly
Cash Flow Projection						
Income and Expense—Overall						
Income and Expense—by Area						
Balance Sheet						
Balance Sheet Ratios						
Staff Turnover						

Other financial information I would like to see:

CH1011.DOC

Form 10-12 Implementation Checklist		Topic: Financial Empowerment
Measurable Outcome	**Deadline**	**Person or Group Responsible**

● CH1012.DOC

D. ☞ HANDS-ON

☞ **HANDS-ON:** Empower staff to do what you need done to decide how to spend your mission reserve. The absolute best way to use this is to decide on your amount of reserves (and you can start today with $500 or $1,000), and then solicit ideas from staff to spend that amount (or some part of it) on *direct service*. Once all the ideas are in, convene a group of line staff members and let them decide which idea(s) should be funded. The key here is to let your line staff make the decision, not you. You get so much more motivation and ownership if you let them spend the money.

☞ **HANDS-ON:** To find the right bank, take the following steps. Find someone who knows the CEO of each of the three or four (or more) banks that you wish to check out. Have that person (let's call him Mike) phone the CEO (let's call her Jan) and inform her of your interest (let's call you Joe). Have Mike say, "Jan? This is Mike. I heard that Joe's organization is looking around for a new bank, and I thought you might want to give him a call, since I know you're always looking for some new customers. He's got an annual budget of around $1.5 million. Just thought you'd like to know."

Now what has Mike done? He's done his friend Jan a favor, and he has not taken any risk by declaring you a good risk. Proving that is your job.

Now you wait and see how far down the organizational chart you dribble. If Jan or her first vice president calls you back and invites you to lunch at the bank to explain their services, you know the bank is interested and will probably treat you pretty well (assuming their prices are competitive). If, on the other hand, you are never called back, or your call is returned by a junior loan officer with $2,500 in personal loan approval authorization, then you have a good idea about what that bank thinks of not-for-profits in general, and of yours in particular.

☞ **HANDS-ON:** Banks will often tell you that your loan is "two over prime." The question to ask is, "Whose prime, and what is it today?" Some banks use New York prime, and some use their own (often inflated over New York by one or two percent). You need to know the rate so that you can make a valid comparison.

☞ **HANDS-ON:** Here's a newsflash. You can have all the money you need to repair and replace capital items. All you need to do is "fund" your depreciation. What this means is that each month you set aside the same amount of cash as is expensed under "depreciation" on your income and expense report. Thus if you show a monthly depreciation of $1,250, you should add that amount of actual cash to a savings or money market account each month. Why? So that when the things you are depreciating (cars, buildings, etc.) wear out, you will have the cash to replace them. Probably not all the cash, as prices do go up, but you'll be a heck of a lot better off than having no cash. Funding depreciation is good management, good stewardship, and very, very logical. But almost no one in the not-for-profit world does it. Why? Because it requires discipline: You've got to learn to save to empower your organization to do more mission later, rather than spend every dime you have now.

Note: Some funders frown on not-for-profits having any savings at all. You don't have the time now to listen to me tell you *all* of my feelings about how stupid this is, but suffice it to say that there is a solution. Put your depreciation savings in a restricted account. You'll have to do this by board action, but it protects the money from all but the most carnivorous funding source.

☞ **HANDS-ON:** When purchasing, consider two things: leasing and maintenance agreements. Leasing may or may not be cheaper in the long run than buying. I know we were all told to own, not lease, by our parents, but there are times where leasing allows you to be more flexible, and it certainly costs less cash up front. It's one of those options you have available, so at least consider it. Maintenance agreements are like repair insurance. You pay a (usually) small premium now, and the item you are purchasing is covered for a period of time (usually three years) beyond the manufacturers' warranty. Check these out. They can be a terrific deal, but read the fine print carefully.

E. FORMS ON THE COMPANION CD-ROM

Form Name	Form #	Workbook Page	File Name	File Format
Financial Empowerment Self-Assessment	10-1	124	CH1001.DOC	Word for Windows
Financial Status Self-Assessment Form	10-2	126	CH1002.DOC	Word for Windows
Management Status Self-Assessment Form	10-3	128	CH1003.DOC	Word for Windows
Income and Expense Reporting Sample	10-4	130	CH1004.XLS	Excel
Blank Income and Expense Form	10-5	131	CH1005.XLS	Excel
Cash Flow Projection Sample	10-6	132	CH1006.XLS	Excel
Blank Cash Flow Projection Form	10-7	133	CH1007.XLS	Excel
Training Checklist— Financial Empowerment	10-8	134	CH1008.DOC	Word for Windows
Estimating the Cash Needs of Growth	10-9	135	CH1009.XLS	Excel
Capital Planning Template	10-10	136	CH1010.DOC	Word for Windows
Financial Reporting Questionnaire	10-11	139	CH1011.DOC	Word for Windows
Implementation Checklist	10-12	140	CH1012.DOC	Word for Windows

F. RESOURCES FOR FURTHER STUDY

Topic: Financial Empowerment

Books

Financial Empowerment: More Money for More Mission, by Peter C. Brinckerhoff, John Wiley & Sons, ISBN 0-471-29692-9, 1998

Streetsmart Financial Basics for Nonprofit Managers, by Tom McLaughlin, John Wiley & Sons, ISBN 0-471-11457-X, 1995

Budgeting for Not-for-Profit Organizations, by David Maddox, John Wiley & Sons, ISBN 0-471-25397-9 1999

Saving Money in Nonprofit Organizations, by Gregory Dabel, Jossey-Bass, ISBN 0-7879-4515-3 1998

Software

A Review of Nonprofit Financial Software: *www.npinfotech.org/tnopsi/finance/fnindex.htm.* The name says it all.

Websites

A Basic Guide to Nonprofit Financial Management: *www.mapnp.org/library/finance/np_fnce/np_fnce.htm.* A really excellent compilation of information and links. Part of the Free Management Site by Carter McNamara.

On-Line Courses

None that I know of at this writing, but by the time you read this, there probably will be five! Go to the broad-based websites noted in Chapter 3 and look for training on-line.

11

A Vision for the Future

A. STRAIGHT FROM *MISSION-BASED MANAGEMENT*

In developing plans, the first thing many managers have to do is to motivate their staff (and often themselves) that the act of planning beyond the current fiscal year is worth the effort and the "time away from doing our jobs." Of course, good planning is part of your job, an essential part of good stewardship. Thus strategic plans, marketing plans, business plans, and other long-term looks at where you want your organization to go are important parts of your mission capability enhancement efforts. Planning forces you to think about the future, about your environment, how you should allocate your resources, and the process itself offers benefits in teamwork, common vision, and ownership in your organization by all involved.

To get you started, here are the key issues for your staff and board to consider.

1. If You Don't Plan, the Only Way You Get Where You Are Going Is By Accident.

What your organization does is way, way too important to have its future happen by whim, or by accident. You already plan annually. It's called your budget. Why not plan for a longer term, such as strategically?

2. The Planning Process Itself Provides an Unparalleled Opportunity to Involve Large Numbers of Important People in Your Organization—If You Are Willing to Put in the Effort.

One of the terrific outcomes of planning can be the gathering of input (and thus ownership) from previously untapped resources in the community. These can include staff, board, funders, donors, community resources, people who use your service directly, and vendors. The process that allows input also builds stronger networks.

B. BASELINE SELF-ASSESSMENT

Form 11-1 Planning Self-Assessment		
Do you have a current strategic plan (3 to 5 years)?	**4**	**–2**
Do you have a current marketing plan?	**3**	**–2**
Do you train any of your staff in goal and objective setting?	**2**	**0**
Are both board and staff involved in the strategic planning process?	**3**	**–2**
Do your plan's objectives include the following:		
Measurable outcomes?	**3**	**–1**
A deadline for completion?	**3**	**–1**
Support for the goals of the plan?	**3**	**0**
A named person or group responsible for implementation?	**3**	**–1**
Do you float drafts of your plan widely both inside and outside the organization?	**3**	**–1**
Does your planning process include the people you serve, the funding sources, and the community?	**3**	**–3**
Do you regularly review progress at implementing the strategic plan at staff and board meetings?	**2**	**0**
Do you hold people accountable for the goals and objectives that they have agreed to?	**2**	**0**
Total of column score Add each column up and put the answer here ➜		
TOTAL SCORE Add total scores from Yes and No columns and put the answer here ➜		

● CH1101.DOC

SCORING ANALYSIS:

34–24 Excellent
23–15 Very Good
14–8 Adequate
Less than 8—You are not getting the benefit you should out of this resource.

For most organizations the place to start planning is with a strategic plan. If you don't have one, start here. If you do, it may well need updating. As you prepare to plan, use the sequences that follow to help organize and speed your work efforts.

C. WORKSHEETS AND CHECKLISTS

Form 11-2 Training Checklist Strategic Planning

――	Training Type	For Which Staff	Deadline	Responsible Person
	Communications	All		
	Supervision	All Supervisors		
	Goal and objective setting	Planning Committee		
	Facilitating group discussions	Planning Committee members		

⬤ CH1102.DOC

Form 11-3 Planning Checklist

The checklist is divided into the planning phases noted in *Mission-Based Management*.
Go through each phase and assign actions that you feel are needed to answer the questions included.

Phase	Action	Due Date	Person Responsible
Preparedness	Do we have the skills and people necessary to do the plan?		
	Do we have a commitment from administration and our planning committee to allocate the needed time for the plan?		
	Do we have a common purpose for the plan?		
	Do we have the funds necessary to pay for any needed facilitation, surveying, etc?		
	Do we have a deadline for plan completion?		
	Do we have an agreed-upon process for the plan?		
Retreat	Are we going to include board and staff at the retreat?		
	Do we have a facilitator for the retreat?		
	Do we have a place away from our offices to hold the retreat?		
	Do we have an agenda and necessary outcomes listed for the retreat?		
	Do we have the data we need to hold the retreat?		
	Do we have a commitment from the retreat participants to stay for the entire session?		
Data Gathering	Do we already collect the information we need to set goals and objectives? Can we collate it into understandable form?		
	If we need surveys, of who?		
	If we need focus groups, what kind?		

(continued)

Form 11-3 Planning Checklist *(continued)*			
Draft Goals and Objectives	Are our goals broad statements of intended outcome?		
	Do all of our objectives have:		
	Measurable outcomes?		
	A deadline?		
	A person or group assigned to implement?		
	A clear support of their goal?		
	Have we front-loaded our timeline? Did we put all our goals and objectives into a Gantt chart?		
Outside Comment	Who do we want to include in our distribution for comment?		
	Is there anything confidential or proprietary in the plan that should not be sent out?		
	How long should we give them?		
	Should we include a questionnaire, or just let them comment?		
Final Draft and Adoption	Has our planning committee included the key comments from the community?		
	Have we prioritized our most important goals? Did we develop one-year action steps for these goals?		
	Has our board had enough time to review the plan and adopt it thoughtfully?		
Implementation	Have we allocated the budget to implement the plan?		
	Do we have a one year part of the plan to work with monthly?		
	Do we review the plan status at each staff meeting?		
	Do we review the status of the plan at board meetings quarterly?		

● CH1103.DOC

Form 11-4 Implementation Checklist		Topic: Strategic Planning
Measurable Outcome	**Deadline**	**Person or Group Responsible**

● CH1104.DOC

D. ☞ HANDS-ON

☞ **HANDS-ON:** Having facilitated over 60 retreats, I strongly prefer the evening-morning model over any other. Get your group together for dinner, let them review your planning process, review the mission, and consider what kind of world they will be operating in in the evening. Then quit and socialize. In the morning, the retreat participants will return fresh and ready to set goals and put them into a priority order for you. This model produces better results because it gives people a break, and also allows the staff present to socialize with the board—a key extra benefit.

E. SAMPLE PLAN FORMATS

I've included some outlines of plans to get you started, or to help you revise and update your plans if you already have them. These are templates, ideas that you can use and improve on. Don't be wedded to them if they don't work for your organization. Rather, use them as a starting point.

For each type of plan, I've included my suggestions on the purpose, horizon (how long the plan should look out), and cycle (how regularly the plan should be rewritten), as well as a definition of what the plan should support. Note that the horizon is often longer than the planning cycle. That's intentional. I want you to think long, but rewrite regularly enough to keep abreast of current events.

Strategic Plan

Purpose: *To guide the organization as a whole toward the realization of its mission.*
The Plan Supports: *The Mission*
Planning Horizon: *Five years*
Planning Cycle: *Develop a Strategic Plan every three years, with annual components written every twelve months.*

Strategic Plan Outline

1. Executive Summary
   Key areas of action, priority goals
2. Introduction to the Plan
   Why you developed the plan, how it will be used.
3. The Planning Process
   Who was included, what the process itself entailed.
4. The History of Your Organization
   No more than two pages on your organizational heritage.
5. The Organization Today
   A 3 to 5 page description of your services, clientele, and funders.
6. The World We Will Work In
   A listing of assumptions about the future environment, and how they will affect your organization.
7. Goals and Objectives
8. One-Year Plan
   The priority goals and their objective and action steps for the first year.
9. Time Line
   A visual representation of the goals, objectives, and action steps. Usually called a Gantt or PERT chart.
10. Evaluation and Update Methodology
    How and when you will evaluate progress toward implementation, and when you will revise the plan.
11. Appendices
    Minimal supporting information for the plan.

Marketing Plan

Purpose: *To guide the organization as a whole toward the realization of its mission.*
The Plan Supports: *The Mission*
Planning Horizon: *Five years*
Planning Cycle: *Develop a Strategic Plan every three years, with annual components written every twelve months.*

Marketing Plan Outline

1. Your Mission Statement
2. Executive Summary
   A brief summary of the marketing plan including a list of your target markets, your core competencies, and how they match up with the wants of the markets.
3. Introduction and Purpose of the Plan
   A rationale for the uses of the plan. This section can also include a brief recitation of the planning process and its level of inclusion.
4. Description of the Markets
   A full description of your major markets, their wants, their numbers, and projected growth or reduction in demand from these markets.
5. Description of the Services
   A description of each of your services, including number of people served, service area or criteria for service, and any accreditation that these services may have earned.
6. Analysis of Market Wants
   A review of the surveys, interviews, or focus groups that you do to prepare the plan. The wants of the markets and how they match up to your core competencies should be included here.
7. Target Markets and Rationale
   Out of all your potential markets, you will choose a few priority targets. Describe them here in more detail along with your reasoning for their prioritization.
8. Marketing Goals and Objectives
   The goals, objectives, and (for annual plans) action steps that will get your marketing strategies implemented.
9. Appendices
   Minimal supporting information for the plan.

Business Plan

Purpose: *To guide the organization as a whole toward the realization of its mission.*
The Plan Supports: *The Mission*
Planning Horizon: *Five years*
Planning Cycle: *Develop a Strategic Plan every three years, with annual components written every twelve months.*

Business Plan Outline

1. Title page identifying the business plan as the property of your organization. This cover letter includes your name, address, and telephone number and the month and the year that the plan is written or revised. One paragraph states in simple terms who the business plan belongs to and the limitations on its distribution.
2. Table of contents.
3. Summary of the plan. This should include a brief paragraph about your organization; a four-line description of the product or service; a four-line description of the market; if needed, a brief paragraph on production and one on distribution; and a short paragraph on the financing requirements.

4. Description of your organization and its business with the following subheadings:
   - the organization
   - the product or service
   - the target consumer
   - the consumer's want for the product or service
   - the sales strategy
5. Description of the market for your product or service, including information on the competition and cost price comparisons between competitors and your organization.
6. Marketing plan that includes information on:
   - the markets
   - customers
   - competitors
   - the macro-environment
   - how each of these areas affects the marketing and selling of your product or service
   - evaluation of potential pitfalls
7. Financial plan with sources and applications of cash and capital and:
   - an equipment list
   - a balance sheet
   - break-even analysis
   - cash flow estimates by month for the first year, by the quarter for the second and third years
   - projected income and expenses for the first three years; and notes of explanation for each of the estimates
8. Goals and objectives with a time line.
9. Minimal appendix with:
   - management resumes
   - survey or focus group data from customers
   - other pertinent material about your organization and its work

F. FORMS ON THE COMPANION CD-ROM

Form Name	Form #	Workbook Page	File Name	File Format
Planning Self-Assessment	11-1	145	CH1101.DOC	Word for Windows
Training Checklist	11-2	146	CH1102.DOC	Word for Windows
Planning Checklist	11-3	147	CH1103.DOC	Word for Windows
Implementation Checklist	11-4	149	CH1104.DOC	Word for Windows

G. RESOURCES FOR FURTHER STUDY

Topic: Strategic Planning

Books

Strategic Planning for Public and Nonprofit Organizations, by John Bryson, Jossey-Bass, ISBN 0-7879-0141-5, 1995

Strategic Planning for Nonprofit Organizations: A Practical Guide and Workbook, by Michael Allison and Jude Kaye, John Wiley & Sons, ISBN 0-471-17832-2, 1997

Software

Again, none that I know of beyond standard project software. But by the time you read this. . . .

Websites

Strategic Planning For Nonprofits: *www.mapnp.org/library/plan_dec/str_plan/str_plan.htm.* Another excellent resource from the Free Management Site.

What is Strategic Planning? *www.nonprofits.org/npofaq/03/22.html.* A site from the Support Centers.

On-Line Courses

Learning Institute for Nonprofit Organizations: *www.uwex.edu/li.* The Learning Institute provides live satellite training in a variety of subjects, including boards of directors, strategic planning, fund-raising, marketing, social entrepreneurship, managing volunteers, etc. These courses are being put on the web as well.

12

Controls That Set You Free

A. STRAIGHT FROM *MISSION-BASED MANAGEMENT*

Along with planning, the development of controls is perhaps the most difficult part of your mission-based improvements to get people motivated. After all, forms and policies seem a long way from mission, from fund-raising, or from marketing. But in our ever more litigious society, having controls in place is responsible stewardship. And who ever said that stewardship always had to be fun?

So, here are a few ideas to get you started in this area.

1. Good Controls Let You Sleep at Night.

Controls are designed to set limits, and to keep important functions consistent. They are also important to give people guidance when the CEO is not around. Thus, taking the time to develop, and keep up to date, good controls is a key part of good stewardship. It will allow the management team to manage rather than administer day to day.

2. Good Controls Set Limits and Outcomes Needed. They Should Support the Strategic Plan.

All of us need limits. Set them with your controls and then enforce them. If you aren't willing to enforce a certain part of a policy, don't put it in writing! Make sure your policies are up to date and enforceable.

3. A Good Control Development Process Includes a Wide Number of Staff.

Have a staff committee that looks at your policies with representation from all levels of the organization. Then, make sure that draft policies are floated to give people input and ownership. You will get good practical ideas and less resistance when a policy is implemented.

B. BASELINE SELF-ASSESSMENT

Form 12-1 Controls Self-Assessment		
	Yes	**No**
Do you have the following policies, and have they been updated within the past 24 months:		
Bylaws	**3**	**–3**
Conflict of Interest	**2**	**–2**
Financial Policies	**2**	**–3**
Personnel Policies	**2**	**–3**
Media Policies	**2**	**–1**
Quality Assurance Policies	**2**	**0**
Do you train staff and board annually on key policies?	**2**	**0**
Do you enforce your policies consistently?	**3**	**–2**
Total of column score Add each column up and put the answer here ➜		
TOTAL SCORE Add total scores from Yes and No columns and put the answer here ➜		

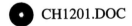 CH1201.DOC

SCORING ANALYSIS:

39–32 Excellent
31–23 Very Good
22–14 Adequate
Less than 14—You are not getting the benefit you should out of this resource.

As you start to deal with this area, pick your most important controls (finance and personnel) and run them through the control development/revision process shown starting with Form 12-2. Then keep going though all the checklists.

C. WORKSHEETS AND CHECKLISTS

Form 12-2 A Control Development/Revision Process			
For each control you develop, try this process.			
——	**Item**	**Deadline**	**Responsible Person**
	Get samples from peer organizations, or from your state or national trade association.		
	Write or amend your policy in draft. Remember to use a staff from all levels of the organization.		
	Float the policy for comment, particularly with those who will use it most.		
	Amend the policy as needed. Get it adopted by the appropriate body.		
	Implement the policy with training for all those affected.		
	Enforce the policy as written!		

● CH1202.DOC

Form 12-3 Control Checklist—Bylaws

___	Item	Deadline	Responsible Person
	Do they include:		
	Your current mission statement		
	Terms of service on the board		
	Specific quorum requirements		
	Dissolution clause		
	Specific restrictions or intentions		
	Are your current bylaws on file with the IRS and your state attorney general or secretary of state?		

● CH1203.DOC

Form 12-4 Control Checklist—Conflict of Interest

___	Item	Deadline	Responsible Person
	Do they include:		
	Bidding required over a certain dollar amount.		
	What board members can or cannot do in terms of bidding or voting on an issue where they may have an outside interest.		
	What the rules are for staff in terms of their families working on contract for the organization?		
	A definition of conflict of interest for board and for staff.		
	Do you train board and staff on conflict of interest annually?		

● CH1204.DOC

Form 12-5 Control Checklist—Financial Policies

___	Item	Deadline	Responsible Person
	Do your policies include:		
	Reports and budgets that specifically focus on cash position of the organization?		
	An annual outside audit and management letter, that is presented to the board?		
	A number of signatures required on checks over certain size?		
	Controls on payables?		
	A written policy on debt?		
	An investment policy for your endowment?		

CH1205.DOC

Form 12-6 Other Controls

___	Item	Deadline	Responsible Person
	Do you have up to date policies for:		
	Media Relations		
	Volunteers		
	Program Provision		
	Quality Assurance		
	Personnel (Human Resources)		
	Disaster Management		

CH1206.DOC

Form 12-7 Training Checklist Controls

____	Training Type	For Which Staff	Deadline	Responsible Person
	Personnel Policies	Human Resources staff		
	Financial Policies	Financial staff, Finance committee, key management staff		
	Media Policies	Public Relations staff		

● CH1207.DOC

Form 12-8 Implementation Checklist   Topic: Controls

Measurable Outcome	Deadline	Person or Group Responsible

● CH1208.DOC

D. ☞ HANDS-ON

☞ **HANDS-ON:** In many of your policies and procedures you will have forms: evaluation, cash receipts, travel reimbursement, timesheets, and the like. Make sure that in every case you include a sample of the form *filled in* as an example. I have yet to see a form and instructions, no matter how clearly written, that were not misinterpreted by someone. Having a filled-in form as an example, in addition to blank ones for immediate use, allows the potential user to have a clear idea of how to use the form. It will reduce frustration and save a great deal of time.

☞ **HANDS-ON:** Policy development is one of the areas where my technique of recruiting a "professional volunteer" works best. The purpose of the recruitment is to get a real expert to look at your problem—in this case your policy, without requiring him or her to a long-term commitment as a board member. What you do, taking your personnel policies as an example, is go to the CEO of your bank, or of another large company that has supported you in the past, and say, "We're reviewing our personnel policies this year and wondered if you had a staff person who could provide us with his or her expertise in personnel issues for 3 to 4 two-hour meetings over the next three months?" Then the CEO gives you the name and feels he or she has made a "donation," the expert gives their time, but doesn't feel saddled with a long-term commitment, you get your expertise for free, and the expert may, in fact, become enamored of your organization and agree to help again, serve in another capacity, or donate to your organization! Try this, it works.

☞ **HANDS-ON:** Don't assume that *anything* is too minute or too obvious to write down! That is why it is so critical to develop these with a group of line staff as well as with managers. I once saw a set of program policies for a health clinic that had such items as the information required on check in, directions on how to offer coffee or tea in the waiting room in English and Spanish, what to do with blood tests, etc., etc., but forgot to direct the nurses to take the temperature and blood pressure of the patient! When a new LPN came on board, she was trained in the policies, and it wasn't until the patient charts were reviewed a week or two later that people noticed that these key items were not being assessed. When asked why not, she said, "You have great procedures, and I was just following them. It didn't make a whole lot of sense, but I'm new and didn't want to make trouble." Don't fall into this trap. Let your staff know that policies are not substitutes for common sense.

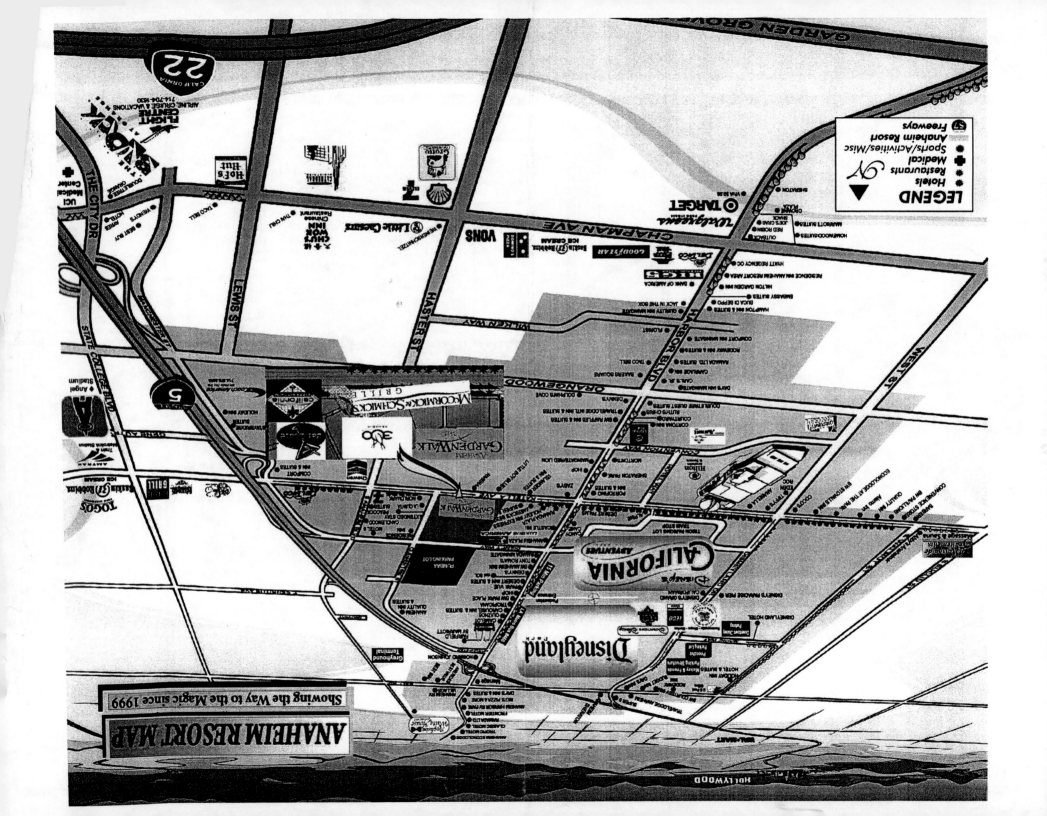

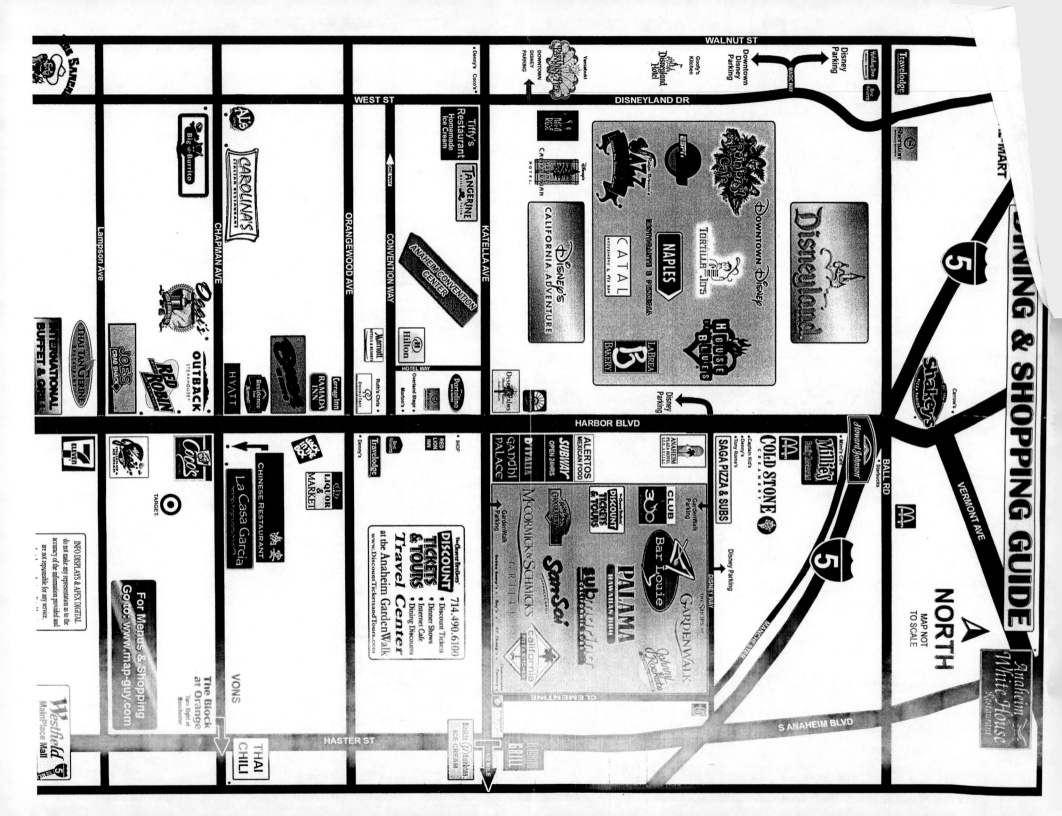

E. FORMS ON THE COMPANION CD-ROM

Form Name	Form #	Workbook Page	File Name	File Format
Controls Self-Assessment	12-1	155	CH1201.DOC	Word for Windows
A Control Development/ Revision Process	12-2	156	CH1202.DOC	Word for Windows
Control Checklist— Bylaws	12-3	157	CH1203.DOC	Word for Windows
Control Checklist— Conflict of Interest	12-4	157	CH1204.DOC	Word for Windows
Control Checklist— Financial Policies	12-5	158	CH1205.DOC	Word for Windows
Other Controls	12-6	158	CH1206.DOC	Word for Windows
Training Checklist— Controls	12-7	159	CH1207.DOC	Word for Windows
Implementation Checklist	12-8	159	CH1208.DOC	Word for Windows

F. RESOURCES FOR FURTHER STUDY

Topic: Controls
Books
Creating Your Employee Handbook, by Leyna Bernstien, Jossey-Bass, ISBN 0-7879-4844-6, 1999
Nonprofit Organization Management: Forms, Checklists and Guidelines, Aspen Publishers, ISBN 0-8342-0710-9, 1994
The Nonprofit Handbook: Management edited by Tracy Connors, John Wiley & Sons ISBN 0-471-17967-1, 1997
Software
Nonprofit Organization's Business Forms, disk edition, John Wiley & Sons, ISBN 0-471-18398-9
Websites
Personnel Policies, Handbooks and Records: *www.mapnp.org/library/policies/policies.htm.* More great stuff from the Free Management Site.
On-Line Courses
None that I know of at this writing, but by the time you read this, there probably will be five! Go to the broadbased websites noted in Chapter 3 and look for training on-line.

Index

Made in the USA